iBOOKS PRO

THE

A NE

(Mainly,

Name: *Son o*

Weight: *very light reading*

Height: *of insanity*

Delivered by: *William M. Gaines and the Staff of Mad*

WHY NOT ADOPT IT FOR YOUR VERY OWN?

Yes, MAD . . . the magazine that brought a new look to the publication field . . . a look of horror . . . proudly presents this brand new bundle of joy . . .

SON OF MAD

Take this baby home with you! Cradle it in your arms and caress its soft, smooth pages! Gather it to your bosom and pat its colicky contents! Then read it . . .

There'll be gurgles after "How to Be Smart" . . .

There'll be gasps after "Wild ½" . . .

There'll be burps after "Talk" . . .

And there'll be plenty of quick changes after "Ganefs," "Let's Go for a Ride," "Miltie of the Mounties" and the rest . . .

By George, YOU'LL need them quick changes!

SON OF MAD is that funny!

Why Sleep

when you can be miserably awake with

THE BEDSIDE MAD

a carefully selected guide to hysteria and insomnia!

Probably one of the greatest contributions ever made to literature, this companion volume to *Son of Mad* is not a book to scorn. You might despise it, but never forget—YOU NEED IT. Don't waste your valuable night hours in sleep. Do something constructive. Read *THE BEDSIDE MAD* to improve your mind. You'll find yourself howling in glee. If your neighbors throw shoes, you can start a new hobby. If you can't buy THE BEDSIDE MAD locally, the New American Library accepts coin (35¢ to cover their exorbitant payment to the editor for his creative efforts, plus 5¢ for the old wrapper the book will arrive in). You could try sending it to them at 501 Madison Avenue, New York 22, N. Y. Who knows, you might get a copy of the book!

WILLIAM M. GAINES'S

SON OF MAD™

ibooks
new york
www.ibooksinc.com

DISTRIBUTED BY SIMON & SCHUSTER, INC

Front cover painting by Kelly Freas

Special thanks to:
Grant Geissman;
Nick Meglin (*MAD* Magazine)

An ibooks, inc. Book

Distributed by Simon & Schuster, Inc.
1230 Avenue of the Americas, New York, NY 10020

ibooks, inc.
24 West 25th Street
New York, NY 10010

The ibooks World Wide Web Site Address is:
http://www.ibooksinc.com

Visit www.madmag.com

ISBN 0-7434-7496-1
First ibooks, inc. printing August 2003
10 9 8 7 6 5 4 3 2 1

Printed in the U.S.A.

CONTENTS

INTRODUCTION
by Grant Geissman

Son of MAD is the seventh book in this series of anniversary reprints of the early *MAD* paperbacks.

The original version of *Son of MAD*—the second *MAD* paperback to be issued under the Signet Books imprint—appeared in October 1959, just six months after the previous book in the series, *The Bedside MAD*. The title *Son of MAD* was inspired by the numerous movie sequels that included "Son of . . ." in their titles, including *Son of Kong*, *Son of Dracula*, *Son of Lassie*, *Son of Sinbad*, *Son of Ali Baba*, *Son of Zorro*, and countless others. The cover of *Son of MAD*—commissioned especially for the book—was rendered by beloved illustrator Kelly Freas, who was the magazine's regular cover artist at the time.

The material appearing here is an interesting mix of pieces that originally appeared in *MAD*'s original incarnation as a 10¢ comic book (1952-1955), and from its earliest issues as a 25¢ magazine (1955-1956). With but a few exceptions, this early *MAD* material was created, written, and laid out for the artists by the triple threat artist/writer/editor Harvey Kurtzman.

Kicking off the book is a classic piece from *MAD*'s

fourth issue as a magazine, "How to be Smart" (*MAD* #27, April 1956, illustrated by Wallace Wood). In the opening text of the article, Kurtzman's self-deprecating humor is clearly evident; this self-deprecation quickly became a hallmark at *MAD* that is still clearly evident in the magazine today, almost fifty years after Kurtzman's departure as its editor. Supporting Kurtzman's wry text is Wallace Wood's tour de force artwork, memorably depicting quintessentially 1950s scenes of cocktail parties, well-decorated *modern* apartments, and employees chatting around the office water cooler. And Kurtzman's words of wisdom at the very end of the article have always seemed to be very sage advice, indeed!

"Kane Keen, Private Eye!" (*MAD* #5, June-July 1953, illustrated by Jack Davis) is Kurtzman's take on the 1950s television detective drama *Martin Kane, Private Eye*. Although obscure today, the show ran on NBC from September 1949 to June 1954. The series went through four different actors in the lead role, which no doubt didn't help its longevity; the best-known actor in the role of Martin Kane was Lloyd Nolan. (Interestingly, Fox Features released two issues of a *Martin Kane, Private Eye* comic book in 1950, with artwork by Wallace Wood.) Another parody of a now somewhat obscure genre is "Miltie of the Mounties!" (also from *MAD* #5, illustrated by John

Severin), which spoofs the crimefighting Royal Canadian Mounted Police, best typified on film by Cecil B. DeMille's 1940 epic *Northwest Mounted Police* (starring Gary Cooper, Paulette Goddard, and Madeleine Carroll), and on radio by *Sergeant Preston, King of the Yukon*, which ran from 1938-1955. (*Sergeant Preston, King of the Yukon* was also represented in comic books, with a series published by Dell that ran from 1951-1959.) It is interesting to note that, at least in some cases, *MAD* has far outlived the objects of its parody!

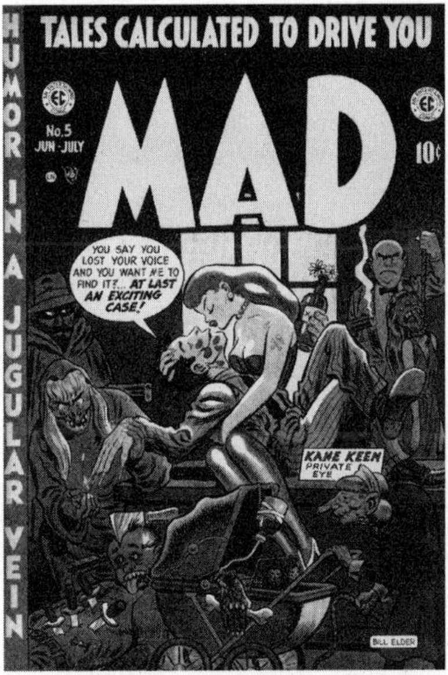
TALES CALCULATED TO DRIVE YOU
MAD
HUMOR IN A JUGULAR VEIN
No.5
JUN-JULY
10¢
YOU SAY YOU LOST YOUR VOICE AND YOU WANT ME TO FIND IT?... AT LAST AN EXCITING CASE!
KANE KEEN PRIVATE EYE
BILL ELDER

The "Kane Keen"-related cover to MAD *#5, June-July 1953, illustrated by Bill Elder.*

"My Secret" (*MAD* #26, November 1955) was both written and illustrated by Al Jaffee, and is a spin on the many articles written by famous golfers on how to improve your game ("Benn Ogen" parodies legendary golfer Ben Hogan). Jaffee did several pieces for the early *MAD* Magazine, then departed with Kurtzman to work on Kurtzman's various worthy-but-ill-fated satire publications, including

Trump and *Humbug*. Jaffee finally returned to *MAD* at the end of 1958, first as a writer, then as a writer/artist, and went on to create two of the magazine's best-known features, "Snappy Answers to Stupid Questions" and the "*MAD* Fold-In."

"Plastic Sam!" (*MAD* #14, August 1954, illustrated by Russ Heath) is Kurtzman's bounce off of *Plastic Man*, the super hero created in August 1941 by writer/artist Jack Cole. In an origin story from 1942, Plastic Man ("Plas" for short) explains to his readers that "an accident left my body in a rubbery plastic state, enabling me to mold or stretch into any shape! Posing as a crook named Eel O'Brian, I live among thieves to get the inside dope on their activities!" Plastic Man's sidekick was named Woozy Winks, who was always attired in the same wacky straw hat, green trousers, and polka-dot shirt. Cole shaped *Plastic Man* into a parody of other "serious" super heroes like *Superman* or *Batman*, which makes Kurtzman's version all the more interest-

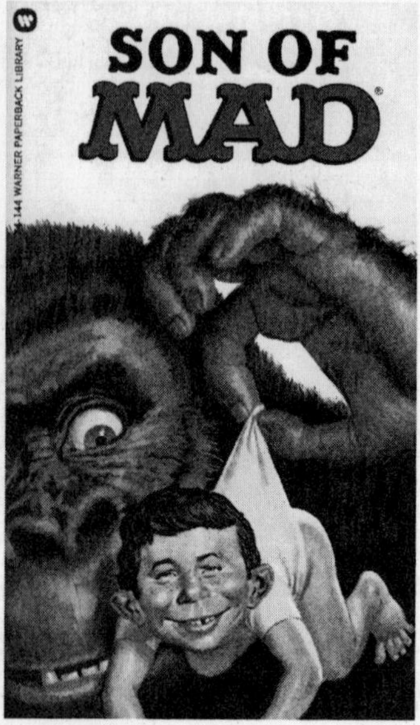
SON OF
MAD
WARNER PAPERBACK LIBRARY

Norman Mingo cover on the 1973 reissue.

ing, being a parody of something that is already a spoof. The artist Kurtzman selected for *MAD*'s parody, Russ Heath, had actually illustrated some episodes of *Plastic Man* for Jack Cole toward the end of the character's thirteen-year run, and since Heath had also done some work on Kurtzman's war comics, no doubt the opportunity to use him on "Plastic Sam!" seemed too good to pass up. Kurtzman always provided tissue paper layouts of each story for the artists to follow; usually the artists referred to the layouts but worked within their own style. Heath chose to follow Kurtzman's layouts precisely, almost as if he had simply inked right over Kurtzman's pencils, and the effect is striking: you can clearly observe Kurtzman's original vision of the story, even though the actual artwork is Heath's.

The two pieces listed in the contents page under the heading "Scenes We'd Like to See" are actually unrelated. The first, "One Against Four," is from *MAD* #31 (January-February 1956), its eighth issue as a 25¢ magazine; the second, "Let's Go for a Ride," is from *MAD* #26 (November 1955). "One Against Four" was both written and illustrated by Phil Interlandi, who did about nine of these "Scenes We'd Like to See" pages before going on to a long career as a cartoonist for *Playboy*. "Let's Go for a Ride" was written by Kurtzman and illustrated by Jack Davis. Davis is here in all his

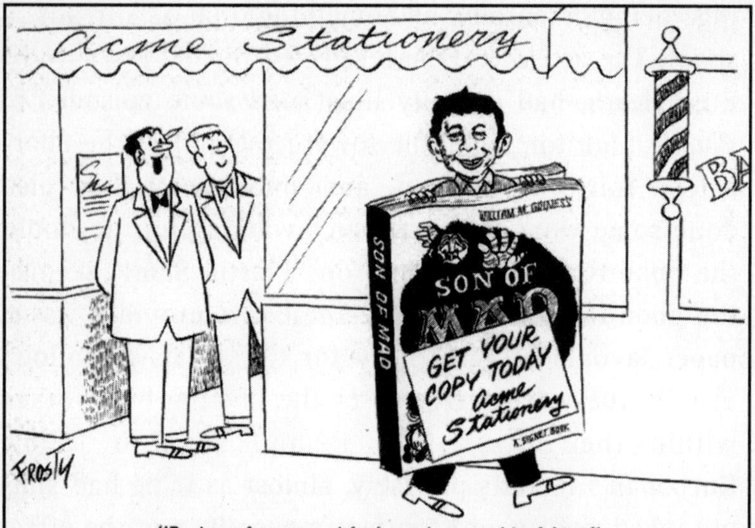
Acme Stationery
BA
WILLIAM M. GAINES'S
SON OF MAD
SON OF
GET YOUR
COPY TODAY
Acme
Stationery
A SIGNET BOOK
FROSTY

"Business has sure picked up since we hired him."

Son of MAD *cartoon from the November, 1959 issue of the defunct industry trade publication* Newsdealer.

cross-hatched glory; especially notable are the splash panel of the family on the porch at home (found here on page 76), and the chaotic panel of the picnic grounds (page 87).

"Wreck of the Hesperus" (*MAD* #16, October 1954, illustrated by Wallace Wood) is the first *MAD* skewering of an H. W. Longfellow classic; "Paul Revere's Ride" would follow several issues later. Kurtzman tackled a number of other poetic evergreens in the *MAD* comic book, including Edgar Allan Poe's "The Raven," H. Antoine D'Arcy's "The Face Upon the Floor," and E.

L. Thayer's "Casey at the Bat." For these treatments, Kurtzman would transfer the original verse to the art boards, provide a tissue paper layout for the artist to follow, and then stand back and watch the fun.

"Wild 1/2" (*MAD* #15, September 1954, illustrated by Wallace Wood) lampoons *The Wild One*, the 1953 movie vehicle starring Marlon Brando. *The Wild One* was actually based on a real-life event in Hollister, California where two rival motorcycle gangs briefly took over that small town. Wallace Wood turns in an inspired performance here, providing a wonderful caricature of the pouty Marlon Brando, as well as page after page of his trademarked moodily lit and zipatoned panels. For his part, Kurtzman uses this story to turn the "bad biker boy" stereotype on its ear.

"Cartoon Digest" (*MAD* #27, April 1956, illustrated by Bill Elder) consists of Kurtzman parodies of various daily newspaper strips of the time, including "Little Orphan Annie," "Mutt and Jeff," "Li'l Abner," "Rex Morgan, MD," "Archie," and "Popeye." As we have come to expect, Elder here is a master mimic, effectively aping the diverse art styles of each of these various strips.

"Ganefs!" (*MAD* #1, October-November 1952, illustrated by Bill Elder) is the only story to appear in a *MAD* paperback to be reprinted from *MAD*'s very first issue. The four stories contained in *MAD* #1 were essentially loose genre parodies of many of the types of stories that were published in E.C.'s other comics, including horror, science fiction, and crime. "Ganefs!" is a generic crime spoof, replete with crime boss, bumbling assistant, and Kurtzman's phonetic spelling of a tough New York accent ("Den we goes to Toid an' Main Street," mumbles Bumble). "Ganef," incidentally, is Yiddish for thief, scoundrel, or rascal.

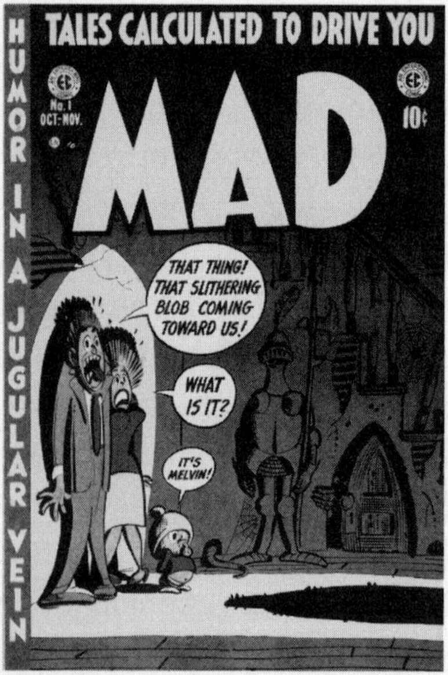
TALES CALCULATED TO DRIVE YOU
MAD
HUMOR IN A JUGULAR VEIN
No. 1 OCT-NOV.
10¢
THAT THING! THAT SLITHERING BLOB COMING TOWARD US!
WHAT IS IT?
IT'S MELVIN!
The Kurtzman-illustrated cover to MAD *#1, October-November 1953.*

Concluding the book is "Talk" (*MAD* #28, July 1956, illustrated by Wallace Wood), which is loosely related in style to the first story in this book, "How to be Smart." "Talk" is one of Kurtzman's "side by side" comparisons, this one comparing "what it *looks* like they're saying" with "what they are *really* saying." Wallace Wood is at the peak of his powers here; Wood's depictions of well-endowed women are without peer!

Coming up next from ibooks is a facsimile edition

of *The Organization MAD*, originally published in April 1960. *More* vintage *MAD*ness is coming your way! Gosharootie!

Grant Geissman *is the author of* Collectibly MAD, *(Kitchen Sink Press, 1995), and co-author with Fred von Bernewitz of* Tales of Terror! The EC Companion *(Gemstone/Fantagraphics, 2000). He compiled and annotated the "best of" volumes* MAD About the Fifties *(Little, Brown, 1997),* MAD About the Sixties *(Little, Brown, 1995),* MAD About the Seventies *(Little, Brown, 1996), and* MAD About the Eighties *(Rutledge Hill Press, 1999). He also compiled and wrote liner notes for* MAD Grooves *(Rhino, 1996), contributed the introduction to* Spy vs. Spy: The Complete Casebook *(Watson-Guptill, 2001), and wrote the introductions to the anniversary editions of* The MAD Reader, MAD Strikes Back!, Inside MAD, Utterly MAD, The Brothers MAD, *and* The Bedside MAD *(ibooks, 2002-2003). When not reading* MAD, *Geissman is a busy Hollywood studio guitarist, composer, and "contemporary jazz" recording artist, with 11 highly regarded albums released under his own name.*

EDUCATION DEPT.

THE FOLLOWING HAS BEEN PAINSTAKINGLY PREPARED BY
OUR FAR RANGING RESEARCH AND SURVEY STAFF FROM A
MULTITUDE OF CAREFULLY ORGANIZED FACTS HE HAS
COLLECTED IN HIS COMPOSITION BOOK FOR THIS ARTICLE:

HOW TO BE SMART

ontrary to our usual policy and all kidding aside, this is going to be a very serious and useful article.

All kidding aside.

Now many people are under the impression that the world is a pretty dumb place and there aren't many smart people around nowadays. To foolishly say whether there *are* lot's of those dumb people will not be the purpose of this article.

To *help* all those millions of dumb people will be the purpose of this article.

And with smartness in the minority, let's face it...you are probably one of 'those'...

Especially since you're reading this magazine.

However, cheer up. You too can be smart. It's easy.

For instance, what makes a person smart? Is it because you *think* you're smart?

Naaah!

Everyone thinks they're smart. ...don't mean a thing.

What makes you smart is when *other* people think you're smart... when they see you passing and say, 'He look smart.' and throw rocks.

The point is...it's how you *look* that makes you smart.

That's where we come in.

On the following pages we will show you in a matter of minutes, how you can look and act so that everyone will think you are smart, making you, in effect, smart.

"Make me smart in a matter of minutes?" you say, "ridiculous!"

See, we say, you are getting smart already.

how to look smart

What a college education accomplishes in years,
a well-chosen adornment can do in minutes . . .

if a loutish look is yours, the condition can be reversed by plain use of heavy black eyeglasses. (glass not necessary.)

with heavy black eyeglasses, loutish looking clod becomes intelligent looking clod.

you can rise above all the other scrub-women with a simple device.

a slender nickel-plate cigarette holder whipped out at the coffee-break will give you that smart look.

9

don't be ordinary, (a sure sign of feeble-mindedness). like for instance, don't wear ordinary cuff-links.

wear cuff-links made out of old coffee grinders.

if you have the ignoramus look of the rest of the pool-hall crowd, an intelligent gleam is yours for the taking.

grow a well-trimmed beard. it will get you out of that pool-hall class …it will get you out of that pool-hall. they'll never let you back in.

Odd clothing, a strange textured jacket, cleverly fastened drop seat, create smart impressions.

just think when you enter the cocktail party, how smart you'll look...

with your fluorescent pink weskit, hand- woven wood-pulp skirt, etc.

or else, you're back outside the elegant party and this time you come in... with faded dungarees, surplus army sweat-shirts and basketball shoes!

or else, you're back outside, and now you create the biggest impression of all. you come in *naked*.

13

how to act smart

Sitting is important in standing out. Outstanding sitting will sit you in good standing . . . er avoid chairs. fling yourself down upon the floor in a gracefully flung posture

there is nothing as smart looking as a flinged figure that is gracefully flung

Carefully chosen words make meaningless conversation, intelligent meaningless conversation.

'fantastic' is a high-class smart word. if your boy-friend wiggles his ears,
don't say: ...say:

Hey! Ya wigglin' ya ears!
Fantastic!

'fabulous' is good. when your neighbor's son shows you his frog collection,
don't say: ...say:

Very inneresting!
Fabulous!

it's smart to use the word 'darling' whether at the cocktail party or the meat market,

don't say: ...say:

Hiya, Mr. Flausglotten.
Daarling!

Cultivate a withering sneer.

practice this sneer. try it on your friends.

Say didja listen to Eddie Fishie's latest pop record, huh? didja? didja huh? didja?
Pop' records?
. . . who listens to (ech) pop' records?

Say didja see the "Krafco Theatre" on television last night? Didja? huh? didja? huh?
Television?
... who watches (yech) television?
HELP!

TO SUM IT ALL UP...to be smart, *be different*. If the others order peanut butter sandwiches, you ask for Pizza. If everyone stands on line, you sneak around the other way. If they talk about the U.S., you tell them about Paris. If they happen to be worldly, you tell them you're a Martian. Yes, you will be very impressive if you can tell them you're a Martian.

Finally...if after reading this article, you are satisfied to remain amongst the peasants, don't go making fun of every person who *is* different or

acts like a Martian...   ...he *might really be* a Martian!

23

CRIME DEPT. 1: IN A DINGY TWO BY FOUR OFFICE ON THE MAIN STEM . . . AROUND A BULLET-SCARRED DESK, WELL-PACKED WITH REVOLVERS, SCOTCH, SODA, PRETZELS, ICE . . . BEING CHASED BY A BLONDE SECRETARY, ALSO WELL-PACKED . . . RUNNING WITH TRENCH-COAT COLLAR UP, BELT PULLED TIGHT . . . RUNS . . .

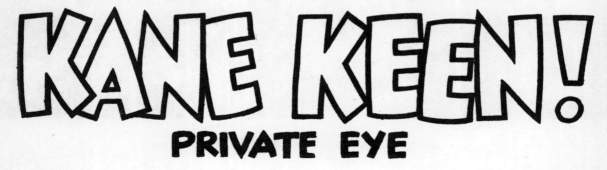

KANE KEEN!
PRIVATE EYE

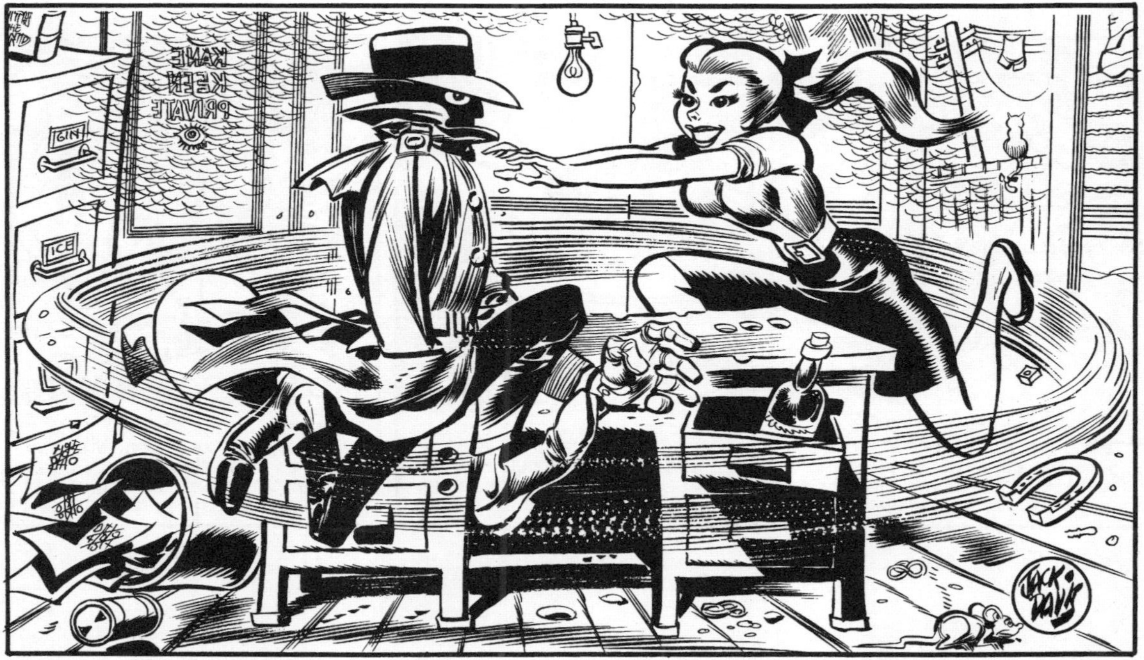
KANE
KEEN
PRIVATE
GIN
ICE
JACK DAVIS

YEAH... THAT'S ME... KANE KEEN, PRIVATE EYE! DOES SOMEONE WANT TO MURDER YOU? DID YOU GET A PARKING TICKET? MY GUN IS FOR HIRE!
THAT'S ME... KANE KEEN!. THE UNDERWORLD HATES ME! THE WOMEN FIND ME IRRESISTABLE! YOU SEE, I USE BURMA-SHAVE!
KLUNK
AT THE MOMENT I AM TRYING TO SHAKE MY SECRETARY WHO HAS BEEN TRAILING ME ALL DAY! ...HAH! A KNOCK ON THE DOOR!
SLERP
NOK NOK

SST! THE DOOR, SWEETHEART! OPEN IT NICE AND EASY LIKE... THEN GET OUT OF THE WAY! I MIGHT HAVE TO PLAY A SYMPHONY WITH A HOT LEAD TEMPO! THEY'VE BEEN LOOKING FOR ME!... JUST **CAN'T** GET RID OF THEM **BILL COLLECTORS!**
KANE
KEEN
PRIVATE
THE DOOR SWUNG OPEN... AND **SHE** WALKED IN... A SYMPHONY IN CHANNEL #5, TABU AND BURMA-SHAVE! AND BY THE SLIGHT BULGE IN HER HAND-BAG, I WOULDN'T SAY SHE WAS FLORENCE NIGHTINGALE!

GAD! ANOTHER BEAUTIFUL GIRL CLIENT! WHY CAN'T AN UGLY OLD MAN COME UP SOMETIMES? WHY ONLY BEAUTIFUL GIRLS?
LISTEN, KANE! MY NAME IS LASSIE ROVER! MY UNCLE IS ROLLOVER ROVER! YOU'VE GOT TO HANDLE MY CASE! MONEY IS NO OBJECT!
YOU MEAN YOUR UNCLE IS ROLLOVER ROVER, THE RETIRED VAUDEVILLE ACTOR WHO HAD THE FAMOUS DOG ACT?
YES! EVER SINCE HE CAME OVER FROM DOVER ON THE GOOD SHIP PLOVER WHERE HE WAS PLANTING CLOVER, HIS LIFE HAS BEEN IN GREAT DANGER!
RING-A-LING

HELLO! KANE KEEN DETECTIVE AGENCY! ALSO NOTARY PUBLIC AND INCOME TAX RETURNS FILLED OUT!
HELLO KEEN?
LISTEN! MY NAME IS ROLLOVER ROVER! I'M GOING TO BE KILLED! MY MURDERER IS... IS...
GET AWAY FROM THAT PHONE...
DROP THAT PHONE!
...IS... IS... IS... IS... IS...
KTOW
BLAM
BLAM
SEE? IT HAPPENS EVERY TIME! JUST AS THEY'RE ABOUT TO TELL YOU WHO THE MURDERER IS... THEY GET KILLT!
2

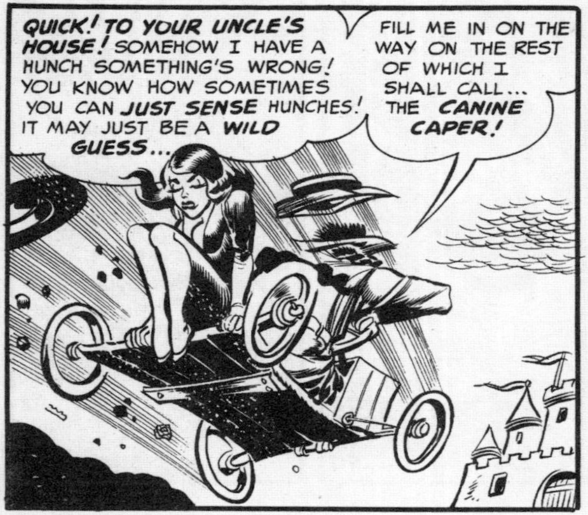
QUICK! TO YOUR UNCLE'S HOUSE! SOMEHOW I HAVE A HUNCH SOMETHING'S WRONG! YOU KNOW HOW SOMETIMES YOU CAN JUST SENSE HUNCHES! IT MAY JUST BE A WILD GUESS...
FILL ME IN ON THE WAY ON THE REST OF WHICH I SHALL CALL... THE CANINE CAPER!

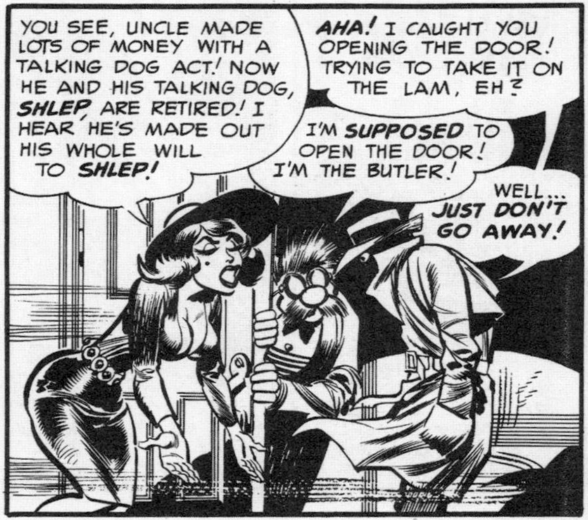
YOU SEE, UNCLE MADE LOTS OF MONEY WITH A TALKING DOG ACT! NOW HE AND HIS TALKING DOG, SHLEP, ARE RETIRED! I HEAR HE'S MADE OUT HIS WHOLE WILL TO SHLEP!
AHA! I CAUGHT YOU OPENING THE DOOR! TRYING TO TAKE IT ON THE LAM, EH?
I'M SUPPOSED TO OPEN THE DOOR! I'M THE BUTLER!
WELL... JUST DON'T GO AWAY!

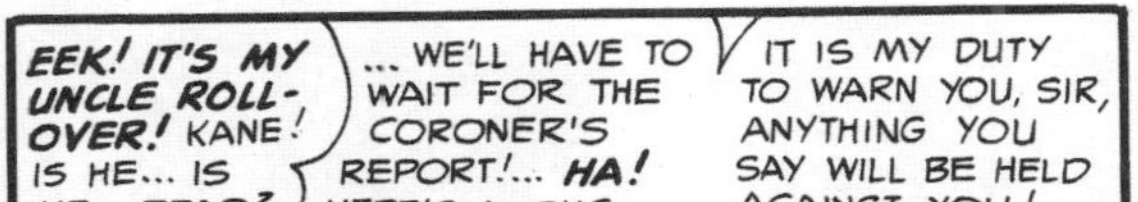
EEK! IT'S MY UNCLE ROLL-OVER! KANE! IS HE... IS HE... DEAD?
... WE'LL HAVE TO WAIT FOR THE CORONER'S REPORT!... HA! HERE'S A SUS-PICIOUS-LOOKING CHARACTER!
IT IS MY DUTY TO WARN YOU, SIR, ANYTHING YOU SAY WILL BE HELD AGAINST YOU! ...JUST DON'T GO AWAY!

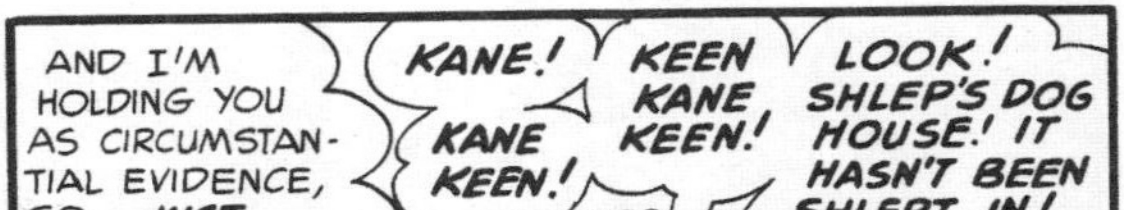
AND I'M HOLDING YOU AS CIRCUMSTAN-TIAL EVIDENCE, SO... JUST DON'T GO 'WAY!
KANE!
KANE KEEN!
KEEN KANE KEEN!
LOOK! SHLEP'S DOG HOUSE! IT HASN'T BEEN SHLEPT IN! SHLEP HAS BEEN KIDNAPPED!
SHLEP'S

AHA! AND SHLEP WAS THE ONE THE MONEY WAS WILLED TO! LIKE A JIGSAW PUZZLE, THE FINE STRANDS ARE COMING TOGETHER!... LIKE A WEB... THE PIECES ARE FITTING INTO PLACE!
HERE SHLEP BOY!
WHERE ARE YA, SHLEP?
OOPS!
HELLO, SHAMUS!
I JUST WANT TO GIVE YOU A WORD OF WARNING!
SHLEP!
SHLEP, OL' BWAH!
COME-A HYAR, SHLEP!
I'M WARNING YOU TO KEEP OFF OF THIS CASE!
CLONG
HOOP
3

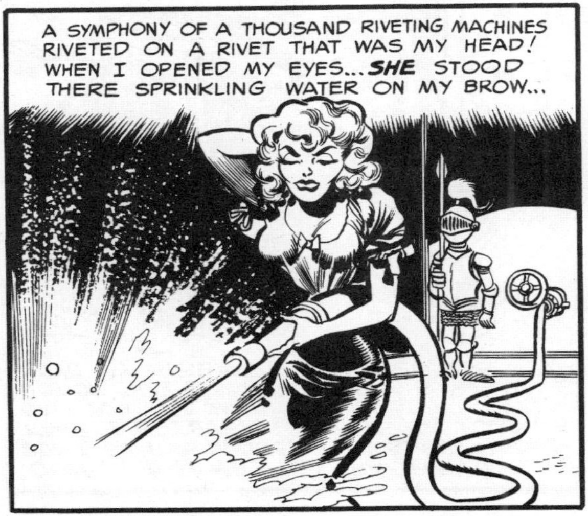
A SYMPHONY OF A THOUSAND RIVETING MACHINES RIVETED ON A RIVET THAT WAS MY HEAD! WHEN I OPENED MY EYES... SHE STOOD THERE SPRINKLING WATER ON MY BROW...

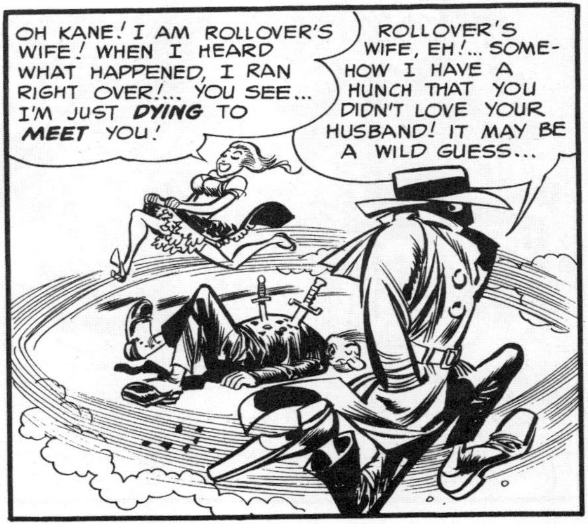
OH KANE! I AM ROLLOVER'S WIFE! WHEN I HEARD WHAT HAPPENED, I RAN RIGHT OVER!... YOU SEE... I'M JUST DYING TO MEET YOU!
ROLLOVER'S WIFE, EH!... SOMEHOW I HAVE A HUNCH THAT YOU DIDN'T LOVE YOUR HUSBAND! IT MAY BE A WILD GUESS...

OOH... HAHAHA! DON'T BE RIDICULOUS, KANE! WHATEVER GAVE YOU THE SILLY NOTION THAT I DIDN'T LOVE MY HUSBAND?
(PUFF, PUFF) JUST A HUNCH! (PUFF) SOMETIMES YOU FOLLOW A HUNCH (PUFF, PUFF) AND IT BLOWS UP IN YOUR FACE!
HA
HA HO
HEE HOO, THAT'S RICH
NOW TO USE SOME COLD AND CALCULATING REASONING TO DEDUCT WHAT DIRECTION I SHALL TAKE NEXT!
PTOO!
HA! I GO THAT WAY!
ALL RIGHT, EVERYONE! STAY WHERE YOU ARE! OPEN UP IN THE NAME OF THE LAW!
CRUNCH

I HEARD THERE WAS A MURDER HERE AND I RUSHED RIGHT OVER!
I RUSHED BECAUSE I WANTED TO BEAT THAT PRIVATE EYE NAMED KANE KEEN! HE ALWAYS GETS TO THE MURDER BEFORE I DO, BUT THIS TIME... THIS TIME...
KANE KEEN, PRIVATE EYE! YOU DID IT AGAIN! YOU BEAT ME TO THE MURDER!
STUPID FOOL! SHVIENHUNT, POLICEMAN! GET OUT OF MY WAY!
WAAH! EVERY TIME THERE'S A MURDER... HE COMES FIRST! ...EVERY TIME!
DUMKOPF! AND KEEP OUTTA MY WAY OR I'LL CALL A COP!
4

I STROLLED THROUGH THE ROVER MANSION LOOK-
ING FOR THE MURDER WEAPON! SUDDENLY ALL
CONCENTRATION WAS BLASTED BY A SYMPHONY
OF LIPSTICK, HIGH HEELS AND A PAIL OF SLOP!

IT WAS THE UPSTAIRS MAID DOWNSTAIRS CLEANING...
CLEANING A COLT 45! I BACKED AWAY...THEN RAN...
NOT FROM THIS BEAUTY! I RAN BECAUSE I HAD
UNWITTINGLY BACKED INTO THE *MURDER WEAPON!*

DANG DANG DANG DANG
OOPS! YOU AGAIN!
SHAMUS! ARE YOU STILL ON THIS CASE!
HEY, SHLEP!
HEY, BWAH!
SHLEPPY!
I'M TELLING YOU FOR THE SECOND TIME... KEEP OFF OF THIS CASE!
WHO CASE? WHAT CASE? WHERE...
HOOP

A THOUSAND HAMMERS PLAYED A SYMPHONY BY SPIKE JONES IN MY BRAIN! I BREATHED A PRAYER THAT NONE OF THE CRACKS IN MY HEAD, FROM PREVIOUS CAPERS, HAD OPENED!
CRASH
HAH! KANE KEEN! I JUST WANT TO TELL YOU YOU'RE NOT SO SMART! I JUST WANT TO TELL YOU I FOUND OUT WHAT THE MURDER WEAPON WAS BEFORE YOU FOUND OUT! BY TEDIOUS DEDUCTION I KNOW IT WAS CAUSED BY A LONG THIN SWORD...
YOU MEAN AN ÉPÉE... A DUELING SWORD LIKE... THIS?!
5

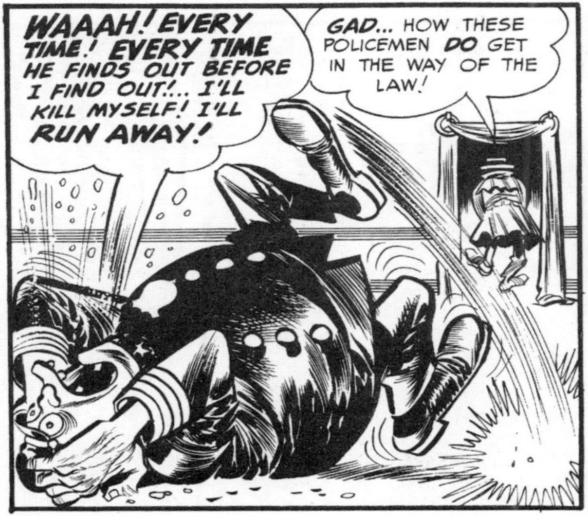
WAAAH! EVERY TIME! EVERY TIME HE FINDS OUT BEFORE I FIND OUT!... I'LL KILL MYSELF! I'LL RUN AWAY!
GAD... HOW THESE POLICEMEN DO GET IN THE WAY OF THE LAW!

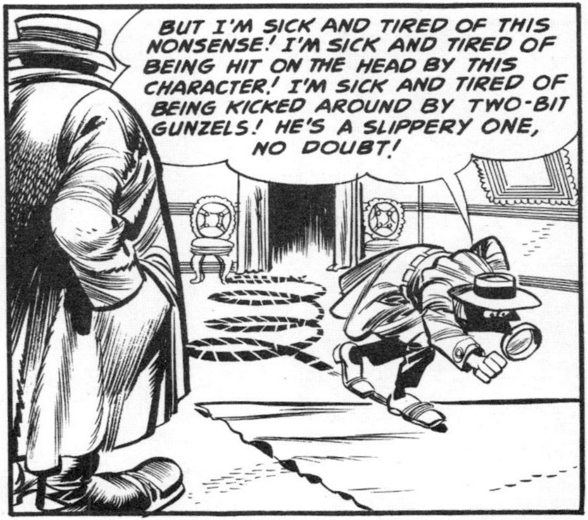
BUT I'M SICK AND TIRED OF THIS NONSENSE! I'M SICK AND TIRED OF BEING HIT ON THE HEAD BY THIS CHARACTER! I'M SICK AND TIRED OF BEING KICKED AROUND BY TWO-BIT GUNZELS! HE'S A SLIPPERY ONE, NO DOUBT!

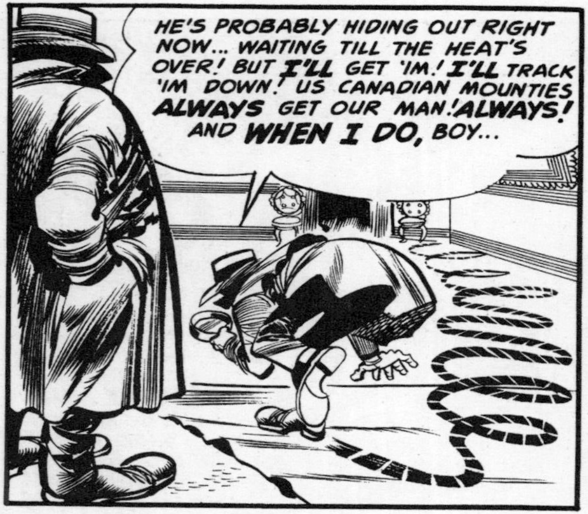
HE'S PROBABLY HIDING OUT RIGHT NOW... WAITING TILL THE HEAT'S OVER! BUT I'LL GET 'IM! I'LL TRACK 'IM DOWN! US CANADIAN MOUNTIES ALWAYS GET OUR MAN! ALWAYS! AND WHEN I DO, BOY...

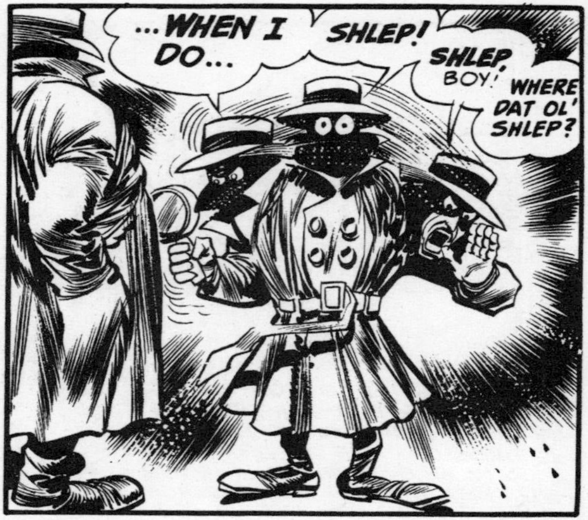
...WHEN I DO...
SHLEP!
SHLEP, BOY!
WHERE DAT OL' SHLEP?

HA! SNAP ON THE HANDCUFFS BOYS! WE GOT 'IM WHERE WE WANT 'IM! TYPE UP A CONFESSION! HE'LL SIGN IT! HE'S THE MURDERER! HE WANTED ME TO GET OFF THE ROVER CASE!
CONFESSION? MURDER? I'M ROLLOVER ROVER'S LAWYER! I DON'T WANT YOU TO GET OFF OF THE ROVER CASE! I WANT YOU TO GET OFF MY BRIEF-CASE! YOU KEEP STEPPING ON IT!
ONCE AND FOR ALL... GET OFF OF THE CASE!
CLONK
6

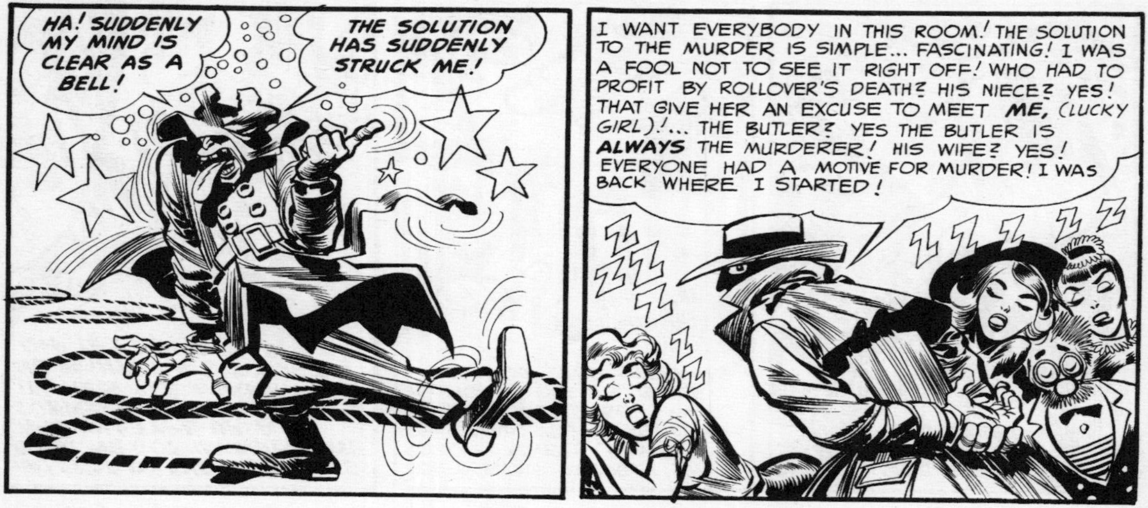
HA! SUDDENLY MY MIND IS CLEAR AS A BELL!
THE SOLUTION HAS SUDDENLY STRUCK ME!
I WANT EVERYBODY IN THIS ROOM! THE SOLUTION TO THE MURDER IS SIMPLE... FASCINATING! I WAS A FOOL NOT TO SEE IT RIGHT OFF! WHO HAD TO PROFIT BY ROLLOVER'S DEATH? HIS NIECE? YES! THAT GIVE HER AN EXCUSE TO MEET **ME,** (LUCKY GIRL)!... THE BUTLER? YES THE BUTLER IS **ALWAYS** THE MURDERER! HIS WIFE? YES! EVERYONE HAD A MOTIVE FOR MURDER! I WAS BACK WHERE I STARTED!
ZZZZ
ZZZZZ

SO I TOSSED A COIN AND IT SHOWED THE MURDERER **WAS** THE BUTLER... WHO IS IN REALITY...
...**SHLEP...** THE TALKING DOG ... IN **DISGUISE!...** SHLEP BEING A RUSSIAN WOLF-HOUND, I RECOG-NIZED HIS ACCENT!
HEY, KANE! THERE YOU ARE! I BET **I** FIGGERED OUT SUMP'N **YOU** DIDN'T!
I FIGURE THE **BUTLER** DID IT!
CRASH

AWRIGHT, EVERYONE! DON'T MAKE A MOVE OR I'LL BITE THIS COP! I'M GETTIN' OUTTA HERE AND NO ONE'S GONNA STOP ME! AND FURTHERMORE... RROWF...ARF...AND BARK!
KANE! DO SOMETHING!
HE'S GETTING AWAY!
STOP HIM!
DON'T BE SILLY, GIRLS! THE 'CANINE CAPER' ENDS RIGHT HERE! THIS ISN'T A CASE FOR DETECTIVES! IT'S A CASE FOR THE DOG-CATCHERS!
7

MY SECRET

Benn Ogen reveals mystery gimmick that made him rich and famous

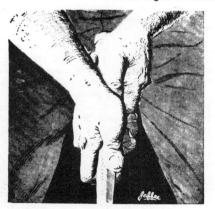

by BENN OGEN

PICTURES BY AL JAFFEE

WITHOUT SECRET Ogen's conventional grip is exactly the same one he has used for years with unspectacular results.

WITH SECRET Ogen shifts his fingers ever so slightly which is the main reason why his opponents could not detect it.

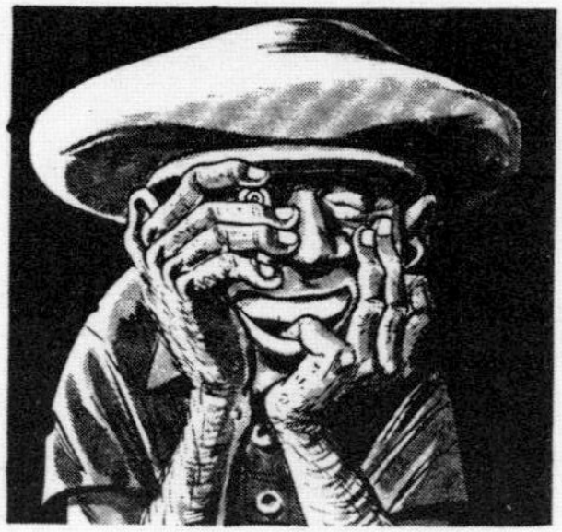

"Tricky lil' Devil, ain't I?"

THE better golfer you become the more trouble you'll have with the hook. A hook is the natural outgrowth of a more powerful swing. It'd be almost funny if it weren't so pathetic to see the ridiculous lengths that some famous tournament players have gone to to get rid of this terrible problem. Take the case of my old friend Sam Snood. Sam approached the problem with calm logic. He figured that since a hook veers off to the left he could solve it by standing a little further over to the right. Little by little he edged further and further over to the right and when the ball was almost landing just right he suddenly developed a terrible slice. Since a slice veers off in the opposite direction of a hook, poor old Sam could do nothing else but start working his way back in the other direction. Just as the slice was about to disappear guess what? . . . that's right . . . the hook returned and with calm logic Sam proceeded to smash every club over his caddie's head. Mang Lloydrum tried various methods of licking the demon hook including a special set of anti-hook clubs with built-in battery-operated swivel heads. A mid-game short circuit ended that idea. Alfred E. Neuman tried the most audacious experiment of all . . . he gave up golf. Oh these poor, deluded boys. I just couldn't help chuckling to myself as I watched their pitiful efforts when all the while (chuckle chuckle) I had the *real* secret. Boy, I just hated myself for laughing at their (HA, HA) expense, but with my secret I was (HO, HO) beating the pants off 'em. They were (HOO, HAH-HA) starving. But now that I'm load—er—now that I've decided to retire I'd like to share my secret with them.

What makes the whole thing so very interesting is the utter simplicity of my secret. I can't understand why no one ever noticed it. You start by simply gripping your club in the usual manner . . . then with a simple motion you start to pronate the right hand till a small "V" is formed between the wrists. Apply the rule about isosceles triangles to this "V" then go on to figure out the distance from angle "A" to angle "B." If it exceeds 11½ degrees, compensate with a simple reverse pronation until left thumb comes right under the middle knuckle of left forefinger. Simple, hey? But wait—that's not the secret yet. You will notice that after all this maneuvering that there's no place to put the right pinky. Well, just point it towards where you'd like the ball to go, then try to hit the ball there.

If it happens—man! *You've* got the *secret!*

THE SECRET BEGINS when Ogen goes into his backswing. He starts his loosening up as shown in picture 2 and continues until he reaches critical moment (3).

Whereupon his left hand pronates downwards (4) with great speed (5).
SECRET CONCLUDES with reverse pronation upwards (6) and a firm

tightening grip (7). Downswing continues till the moment of contact (as in 8) resulting in follow-thru and right pinky pointing to spot ball should light (9).

PLASTIC HERO WORSHIP DEPT.: WHERE ARE THE STRANGE CHAR-
ACTERS OF YESTERYEAR WHO USED TO HAUNT THE PAGES OF
COMIC BOOKS? WHERE HAS THE 'FLASH' DASHED TO? . . . WHERE
HAS 'SUBMARINER' SWUM TO? . . . WHERE HAS 'CAPTAIN MARVEL'
SHAZZAMED TO? . . . THIS STORY, THEN, IS DEDICATED TO THAT
FAST-DYING RACE OF FREAKS . . . TO MEN LIKE . . .

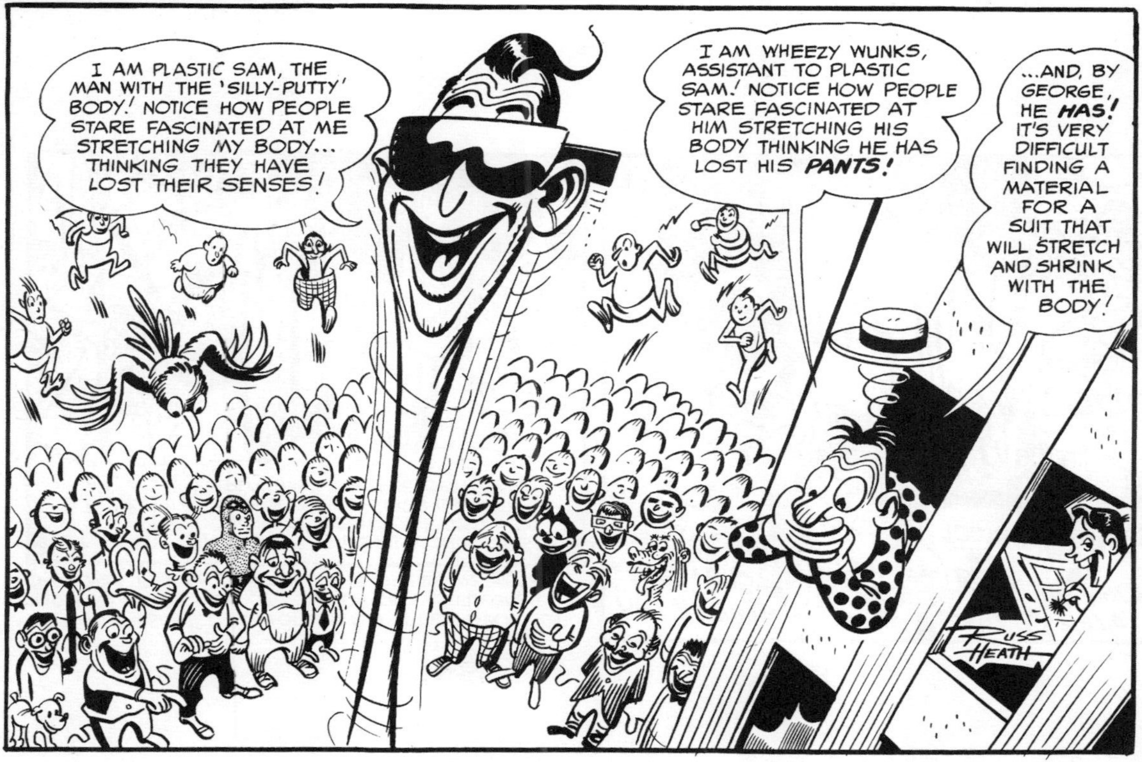
I AM PLASTIC SAM, THE MAN WITH THE 'SILLY-PUTTY' BODY! NOTICE HOW PEOPLE STARE FASCINATED AT ME STRETCHING MY BODY... THINKING THEY HAVE LOST THEIR SENSES!
I AM WHEEZY WUNKS, ASSISTANT TO PLASTIC SAM! NOTICE HOW PEOPLE STARE FASCINATED AT HIM STRETCHING HIS BODY THINKING HE HAS LOST HIS **PANTS!**
...AND, BY GEORGE, HE **HAS!** IT'S VERY DIFFICULT FINDING A MATERIAL FOR A SUIT THAT WILL STRETCH AND SHRINK WITH THE BODY!
RUSS HEATH

OUR STORY BEGINS IN COSMOPOLIS CITY IN THE HIDEOUT OF THIS HERE DIRTY BUNCH OF NO GOOD CROOKS PLANNING TO TAKE OVER THE U.S.A.! AS THE SCENE OPENS, WE HEAR...
... BOYS!... THERE'S ONLY ONE THING IN THE WAY OF US DIRTY BUNCH OF NO-GOOD CROOKS PLANNING TO TAKE OVER THE U.S.A.!!
OW! WATTAYA DOIN', BOSS?
WHY'D YA PULL MY NOSE?
...WHY'D YA BEND MY TOOTH?
WHY'D YA PINCH MY EYE-BALL?

...LIKE I WAS SAYIN', BOYS, THERE'S ONE THING IN THE WAY OF US DIRTY BUNCH OF NO GOOD CROOKS PLANNING TO TAKE OVER THE U.S.A.... AND THAT'S PLASTIC SAM!
HE'S ONE OF THE FEW OF THAT FAST-DYING RACE OF COMIC-BOOK FREAKS LEFT!... HE CAN SHAPE HIS PLASTIC BODY TO LOOK LIKE ANYTHING... LIKE ANY ONE OF YOU BOYS!
...THAT'S WHY I PULLED, BENT, AND PINCHED! NOW I KNOW THAT PLASTIC SAM IS NOWHERE NEAR, NOHOW, NOT, NO, NEIN, NOT... TO DISTURB PLANNING FOR U.S.A. TAKING OVER!
...I DRINK TO OUR PLANNING!
SLURP
TOOEY

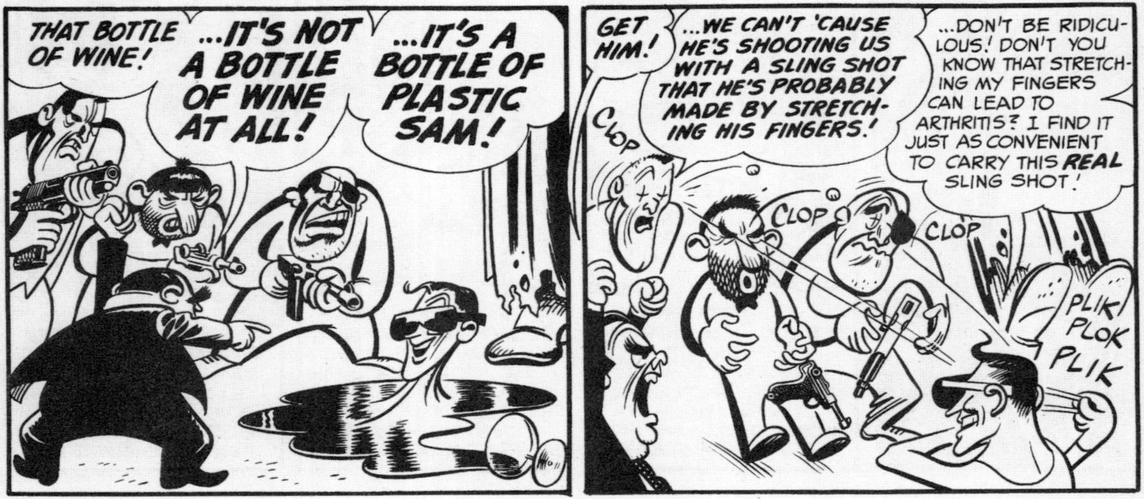
THAT BOTTLE OF WINE!
...IT'S NOT A BOTTLE OF WINE AT ALL!
...IT'S A BOTTLE OF PLASTIC SAM!
GET HIM!
...WE CAN'T 'CAUSE HE'S SHOOTING US WITH A SLING SHOT THAT HE'S PROBABLY MADE BY STRETCHING HIS FINGERS!
...DON'T BE RIDICULOUS! DON'T YOU KNOW THAT STRETCHING MY FINGERS CAN LEAD TO ARTHRITIS? I FIND IT JUST AS CONVENIENT TO CARRY THIS REAL SLING SHOT!
CLOP
CLOP
CLOP
PLIK
PLOK
PLIK

BLAST HIM!
WHERE IS HE?
IN BACK OF THE COUCH!
HEY LOOK!
THE JOINT IS FULLA COPS!
DROP YOUR GUNS!
...NOW I'VE GOT ALL THE GUNS...
...APRIL FOOL!
THE JOINT ISN'T FULLA COPS!
...JUST FULLA FAKE PLASTIC HEADS I WHIPPED UP!
2

WELL, PLASTIC SAM...YOU DID IT AGAIN!
...YOU KNOW THE PLOT YOU HAD IN YOUR LAST ADVENTURE? ...WELL YOU DID IT AGAIN!
YES!...I KNOW!... WIZZY WOONKS, MY ASSISTANT AND SCRIPT WRITER HAS BEEN RUNNING OUT OF IDEAS LATELY! I'M WAITING FOR HIM NOW FOR THE SCRIPT TO MY NEXT ADVENTURE!
PLASTIC SAM! HERE I AM!
I'M SORRY I'M LATE, PLASTIC! I GOT INTO A DISCUSSION WITH LOATHAR AT THE "HEROES' ASSISTANT'S CLUB" I BELONG TO!
...HAVE A STICK OF GUM?
THANKS, WOWZY!
PHOO... THESE ADVENTURES ARE WEARING ME OUT! ...EVERYDAY IT'S GETTING HARDER TO SNAP BACK INTO SHAPE!... EVEN 'STANBACK' DON'T WORK!

...NOW, AS FOR THE SCRIPT... I THOUGHT WE MIGHT USE THE OLD HACK PLOT WHERE A CROOK DISGUISES HIMSELF LIKE **YOU**...
HMM!... IT HAS TO BE CHEWED OVER A WHILE, FIRST! ...MAYBE IF WE KICKED IT AROUND...
...WELL... THE PLOT IS PRETTY SIMPLE...! ...CROOK **DISGUISED** AS YOU, ROBS BANKS! THEY THROW **YOU** IN JAIL... YOU ESCAPE...
...UMMM... MAYBE IF I CUT IT A LITTLE...
WHAT'S TO CUT? THE PLOT IS SIMPLE! ...YOU ESCAPE... CATCH CROOK...! WHAT'S SO COMPLI-CATED ABOUT THAT PLOT?
...IT'S... IT'S JUST NOT THE KIND OF **THING** I CAN SINK MY TEETH INTO!
O.K. FOR YOU, BOY! ...GO WRITE YOUR **OWN** PLOT!
PLOT?... PLOT? WHO'S TALKING ABOUT PLOT? I'M TALKING ABOUT THIS **GUM** THAT I CAN'T SINK MY FURSHLUGGINER **PLASTIC TEETH** INTO!
...SURE WE'LL USE YOUR PLOT!

SO SURE ENOUGH MEANWHILE AT THE COSMOPOLIS BANK...
COSMOPOLIS BANK
POW
SWAG
STOP THIEF!
HE ROBBED THE BANK!
IT'S PLASTIC SAM!
HOW DO YOU KNOW?
I RECOG-NIZE HIM FROM A COMIC BOOK!
AFTER HIM!
3

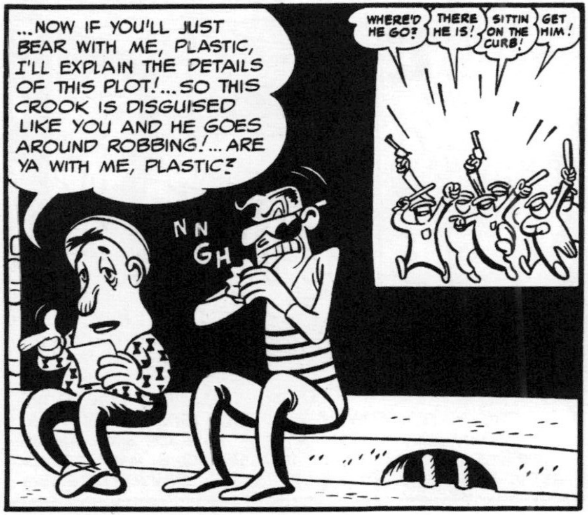
...NOW IF YOU'LL JUST BEAR WITH ME, PLASTIC, I'LL EXPLAIN THE DETAILS OF THIS PLOT!...SO THIS CROOK IS DISGUISED LIKE YOU AND HE GOES AROUND ROBBING!...ARE YA WITH ME, PLASTIC?
WHERE'D HE GO?
THERE HE IS!
SITTIN ON THE CURB!
GET HIM!
NNGH

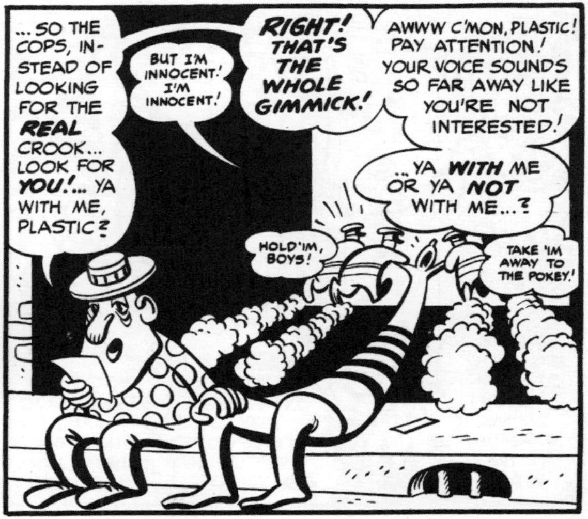
...SO THE COPS, INSTEAD OF LOOKING FOR THE **REAL** CROOK... LOOK FOR **YOU!**... YA WITH ME, PLASTIC?
BUT I'M INNOCENT! I'M INNOCENT!
RIGHT! THAT'S THE WHOLE GIMMICK!
AWWW C'MON, PLASTIC! PAY ATTENTION! YOUR VOICE SOUNDS SO FAR AWAY LIKE YOU'RE NOT INTERESTED!
...YA **WITH** ME OR YA **NOT** WITH ME...?
HOLD 'IM, BOYS!
TAKE 'IM AWAY TO THE POKEY!

WE'RE *FLINGING* YOU IN JAIL, PLASTIC SAM, BECAUSE YOU BROKE YOUR SOLEMN DEMOCRATIC TRUST...BE-CAUSE YOU COMMITTED THE CARDINAL SIN AGAINST HUMANITY... BECAUSE YOU BETRAYED YOUR FELLOW MAN!

...AND MAINLY BECAUSE WE LIKE THE *SPLAT* YOU MAKE WHEN WE *FLING* YOU IN JAIL!

CLANG!

WATCH OUT THAT PLASTIC SAM DON'T TRY TO OOZE UNDER THE DOOR!

...LOOK! HE'S DRIBBLING OUT AGAIN! ...I'LL JUST TROMP THAT DRIBBLE LIKE *THIS!*

WWOOOOOO

I'M WUZZY WURNKS AND I HAVE A PASS TO VISIT THE PRISONER!

TROMP!

O.K., PLASTIC SAM!...I'M LETTING IN A VISITOR, BUT DON'T TRY ANYTHING... 'CAUSE I KNOW YOUR TRICKS!... I KNOW HOW YOU CAN TURN INTO THINGS!
...I KNOW HOW YOU CAN SHAPE YOUR BODY INTO DIFFERENT ANIMAL, VEGETABLE AND MINERAL SHAPES (HE MUST BE JELLY 'CAUSE JAM DON'T SHAPE LIKE THAT)!
I KNOW HOW YOU CAN SHAPE YOUR BODY INTO DIFFERENT HUMAN BEINGS! I KNOW HOW YOU CAN EVEN SHAPE YOURSELF LIKE ME! I AIN'T NO FOOL!
4

...YOU CAN'T FOOL ME, PLASTIC SAM, 'CAUSE *I* KNOW HOW YOU CAN PROBABLY EVEN SHAPE YOURSELF LIKE WOZZY WANKS HERE, WHO JUST WENT OUT THE DOOR!
...JUST WENT OUT THE DO-OR?
I'D LIKE TO TAKE A MOMENT TO EXPLAIN THAT THE TWO-HEADED IMAGE IN THE PRECEDING PANEL REPRESENTS A 'DOUBLE-TAKE' CONNOTING SURPRISE... DISBELIEF!... LET US GO THROUGH IT AGAIN ONCE MORE, SHALL WE?
...JUST WENT OUT THE DO-OR?

PLASTIC SAM HAS ESCAPED DISGUISED AS WAZZY WUNKS!
WAIT! WAIT WAIT WAIT!
LOOK AT THE ARMS!... LOOK AT THE LEGS!... THAT SHAPELESS GOOEY MASS ON THAT COT COULD ONLY BE PLASTIC SAM!
WAIT! WAIT WAIT! WAIT WAIT WAIT WAIT! (GAGG!)
LOOK AT THE TEETH!... LOOK AT THE FILLINGS!... TH-THAT SHAPELESS GOOEY MASS ON THAT COT (GAGG!) COULD ONLY B-BE WEZZY W-W-WONKS (GAGG)!

TOO BAD I HAD TO DO OLD WONK'ZY WEZZ IN, BUT I JUST **HAD** TO GET OUT TO PROVE MY INNOCENCE!
NOW...IF I SHAPE MYSELF LIKE A LAMP-POST, AND HANG AROUND THE BANK... THE CROOK IS BOUND TO SHOW UP...
...ONLY ONE PROBLEM!...WHEN IT GETS DARK... HOW DO I TURN ON THE LIGHT!
COSMOPOLIS BANK
UH-OH! ...ANOTHER PROBLEM!
SCAT
SCAT
AMSCRAM
SCRAM
WOOPS! ...THERE GOES IMITATION PLASTIC SAM!
...NOW TO FOLLOW HIM IN SOME OTHER DISGUISE!
COSMOPOLIS BANK
5

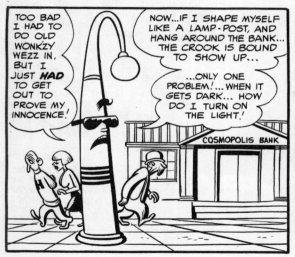

O.K., YOU **YOU** YOU! ALTHOUGH YOU ARE DISGUISED AS PLASTIC SAM, I KNOW YOU ARE IN DISGUISE SINCE **I** AM PLASTIC SAM... IN DISGUISE!
...UH OH!... YOU MEAN YOU **KNOW** MY DISGUISE BECAUSE ALTHOUGH YOU ARE IN DISGUISE, I AM DISGUISED AS **YOU**... RATHER, I AM DISGUISED AS YOU UNDISGUISED?
TELLER
...HA, PLASTIC SAM... YOU ARE DISGUISED AS A BEAUTIFUL GIRL 'CAUSE YOUR PSYCHOLOGY IS I WON'T HIT A BEAUTIFUL GIRL!... RIGHT, PLASTIC SAM?... RIGHT?... RIGHT?
...WRONG!... I GOT MUCH BETTER PSYCHOLOGY AND AM DISGUISED AS BEAUTIFUL GIRL'S TIGHT FITTING COAT!
TELLER

AND NOW, PLASTIC SAM STRIKES! LEMME THINK UP SOME JAZZY COMIC-STRIP STATE-MENTS TO MAKE WHILE PUNCHING VILLAIN...
...LEMME SEE NOW... UMM...
...ONE, TWO THREE STRIKES! YOU'RE OUT!
...TRY THIS ONE ON FOR SIZE...
...PARDON MY KNUCKLES!
SPLAT
SPLAT
SPLAT
SPLAT
CONTRARY TO POPULAR BELIEF, PLASTIC SAM, YOU HAVE NO ABILITY TO PUNCH VILLAIN! SINCE YOUR BODY HAS A CONSISTENCY SOMEWHERE BETWEEN WINDOW-PUTTY AND OATMEAL... AND YOU HAVE NO RIGID BONE STRUCTURE, YOU MIGHT AS WELL HIT ME WITH A WET BEAN-BAG AS WITH YOUR SQWUSHY OLD FIST!
TELLER

AS A MATTER OF FACT, DESPITE YOUR ELASTICITY, YOU **SHOULD** BE **QUITE VULNERABLE...** MUCH LIKE A RUBBER BALLOON...
...ONE HAS MERELY TO TAKE A PINCH OF YOUR FLESH... STRETCH AND SUCK A POCKET INTO IT...
SLURP!
...PINCH THE POCKET CLOSED FORMING A SMALL BUBBLE WHICH, BY TWISTING, BECOMES TIGHTER AND TIGHTER...
...AND THEN IT IS AN EASY MATTER TO SQUEEZE THE BUBBLE AND MAKE IT BURST, CAUSING A RUPTURE IN YOUR FLESH!
POP!
6

...LOOK WHAT YOU DID!... NOW I'M BLEEDING!
...BY GEORGE! ...PINK RUBBER CEMENT!
'SCUSE US, M'AM, WE'RE POLICE OFFICERS!
WE'D LIKE TO INTRODUCE OUR-SELVES!... THIS IS FRIDAY!
...NO, ED!...IT'S SATURDAY!
NO, JOE!... IT'S SUNDAY... I'M SATURDAY... YOU'RE FRIDAY!
WE'VE GOT A WARRANT TO ARREST PLASTIC SAM! WE'RE TAKING YOU IN ON A 3-OH-2... SO HURRY UP AND SNAP ON THE RUBBER BANDS, ED, 'CAUSE THE 3-OH-2 IS ABOUT TO LEAVE AND IF WE MISS IT, THERE WON'T BE ANOTHER TRAIN TILL 5-OH-2!
WAIT! THIS IMITATOR ROBBED THE BANKS!... I'M THE REAL PLASTIC SAM!
...NO! THIS IMITATOR ROBBED THE BANKS!... I'M THE REAL PLASTIC SAM!

WE JUST WANT THE FACKS, M'AM... THE FACKS! IF ONE OF YOU CAN PROVE HE'S PLASTIC, M'AM, THEN WE'LL KNOW WHO'S REAL AND WHO'S IMITATION, M'AM! GIVE US THE FACKS!
LOOKA ME! I'M PLASTIC!
OH, JOE... WILL YOU QUIT TALKING LIKE STAN FREBERG!
...SAY! THERE'S A GOOD IDEA! ...THE ONE WHO CAN STRETCH HIS MOUTH THE MOST, WE'LL KNOW HE'S PLASTIC SAM... WE'LL KNOW WHO IS REAL AND WHO IS IMITATION!
... STAND ASIDE, BRITTLE-HEAD!
FLUP!
(GAGG!) HOW SICKENING! NOW WE KNOW WHO IS REAL! NOW WE KNOW WHO IS IMITATION 'CAUSE PLASTIC SAM HAS DRAMATICALLY AND STARTLINGLY PULLED HIS HEAD INSIDE OUT! (GAGG!) (GAGG!)
... WHICH REMINDS ME... HOW'S YOUR MOM, ED?

HEY! WHY ARE YOU RUSHING **ME** OFF? DIDN'T I PROVE I WAS PLASTIC? DIDN'T I PROVE I WASN'T THE IMITATION?
WE'RE RUSHING YOU OFF, M'AM, 'CAUSE FIRST, ANY MINUTE, AN ORCHESTRA'S GOING TO BUST IN HERE WITH **'DOMM-DA DOM-DOMM'**; AND SECOND... BY PROVING YOU WERE PLASTIC, YOU PROVED YOU **WERE** THE IMITATION! EVERY **KID** KNOWS THAT ANYTHING **PLASTIC** IS AN IMITATION OF THE **REAL THING**! **...WE'RE PUTTING YOU IN THE COOLER, MISTER!**
AND SO THEY DID!... THEY PUT PLASTIC SAM IN A SPECIALLY MADE COOLER... WHERE HE IS NOW AS HARMLESS AS A FROZEN MILKY-WAY CHOCOLATE CARAMEL BAR!
7

SCENES WE'D LIKE TO SEE

ONE AGAINST FOUR

All the world's a stage, and all the people merely players

—Cecil B. DeMille

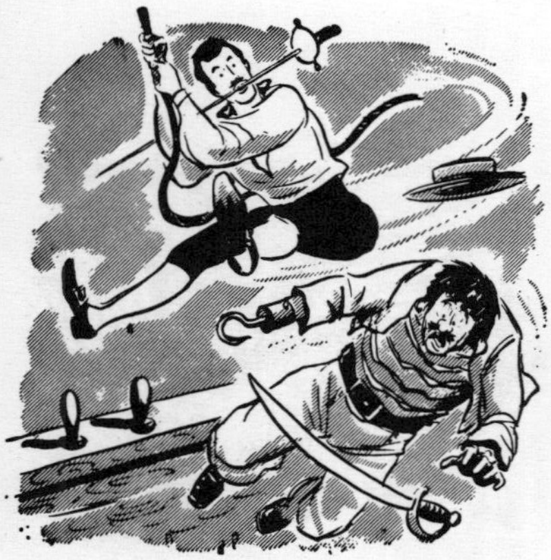

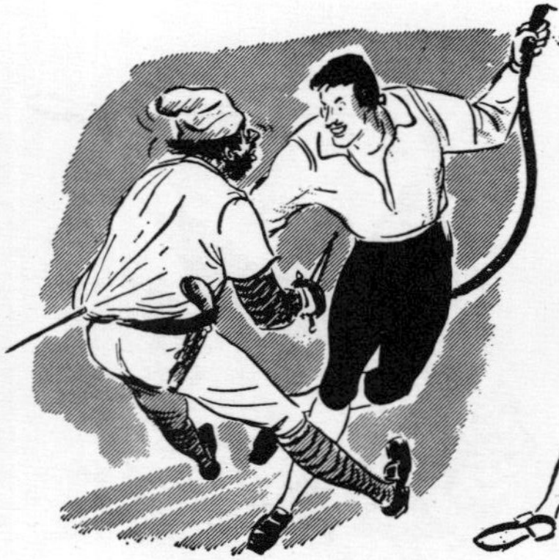

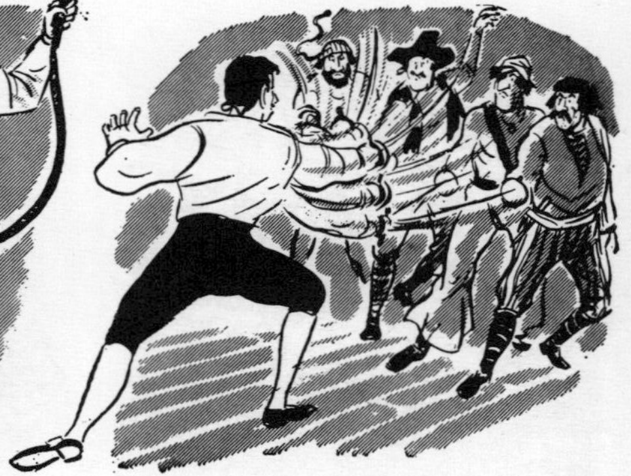

YOU KNOW HOW SOMETIMES YOU SIT AROUND LIKE THIS ON A SUNDAY
AFTERNOON GETTING SO SICK AND TIRED FROM RESTING . . . ?

To enjoy this next article you'd probably have to have a certain amount of experience along the lines we are talking about. In other words, to enjoy this article on 'How-we-live,' you must have mainly lived. And therefore, many won't be able to enjoy this article.

Anyhow, you know how sometimes the family is sitting around on a sunny Sunday afternoon with the Sunday papers, with the baseball game, with nothing to do?

All of a sudden, Pop jumps up and says . . .

LET'S GO

FOR

A RIDE!

Pictures by Jack Davis

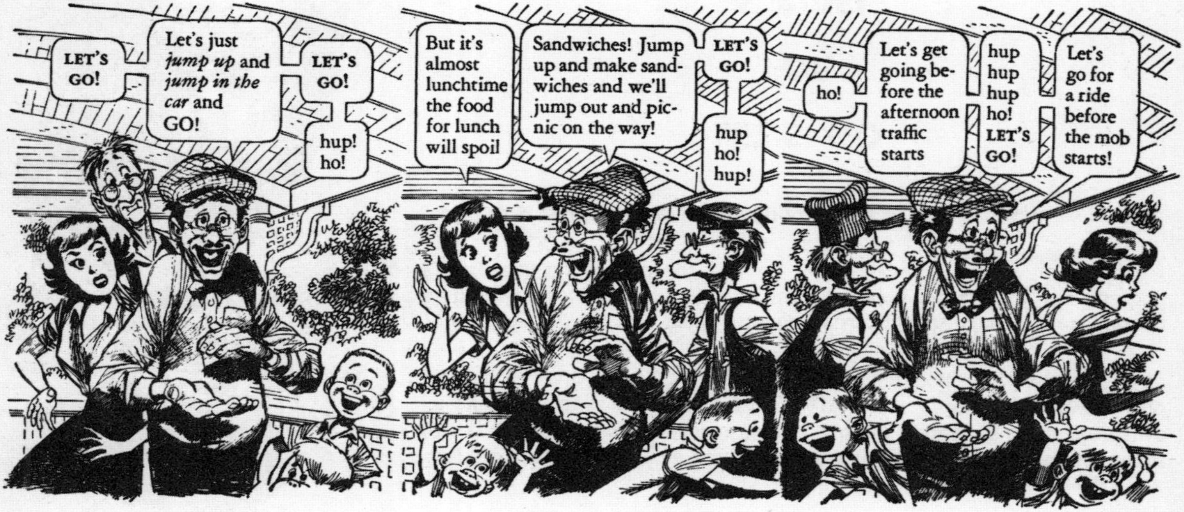
LET'S GO!
Let's just *jump up* and *jump in the car* and GO!
LET'S GO!
hup! ho!
But it's almost lunchtime the food for lunch will spoil
Sandwiches! Jump up and make sandwiches and we'll jump out and picnic on the way!
LET'S GO!
hup ho! hup!
ho!
Let's get going before the afternoon traffic starts
hup hup hup ho! LET'S GO!
Let's go for a ride before the mob starts!

MEANWHILE, just as Pop is saying "Let's go for a ride before the mob starts," like as if you had x-ray vision to look into thousands of homes all over the country, this montage shows what thousands of other people are saying that minute.

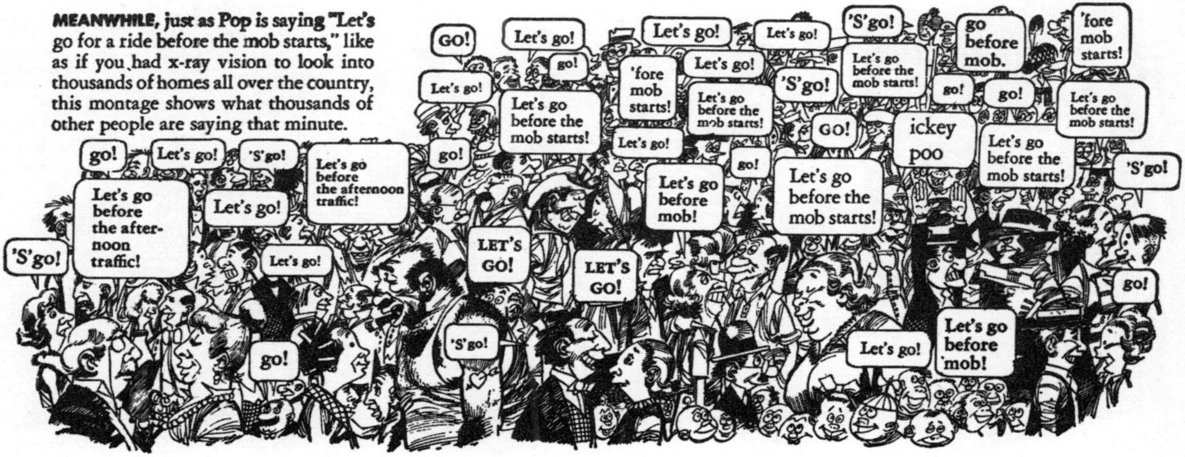

go!
Let's go!
'S'go!
Let's go before the afternoon traffic!
Let's go before the after-noon traffic!
Let's go!
'S'go!
Let's go!
go!
GO!
Let's go!
go!
Let's go!
go!
Let's go before the mob starts!
Let's go!
'fore mob starts!
Let's go!
Let's go before the mob starts!
Let's go!
Let's go!
'S'go!
'S'go!
Let's go before the mob starts!
go!
go!
GO!
go before mob.
'fore mob starts!
Let's go before the mob starts!
ickey poo
Let's go before the mob starts!
'S'go!
Let's go before mob!
Let's go before the mob starts!
LET'S GO!
LET'S GO!
'S'go!
go!
Let's go!
Let's go before mob!
go!

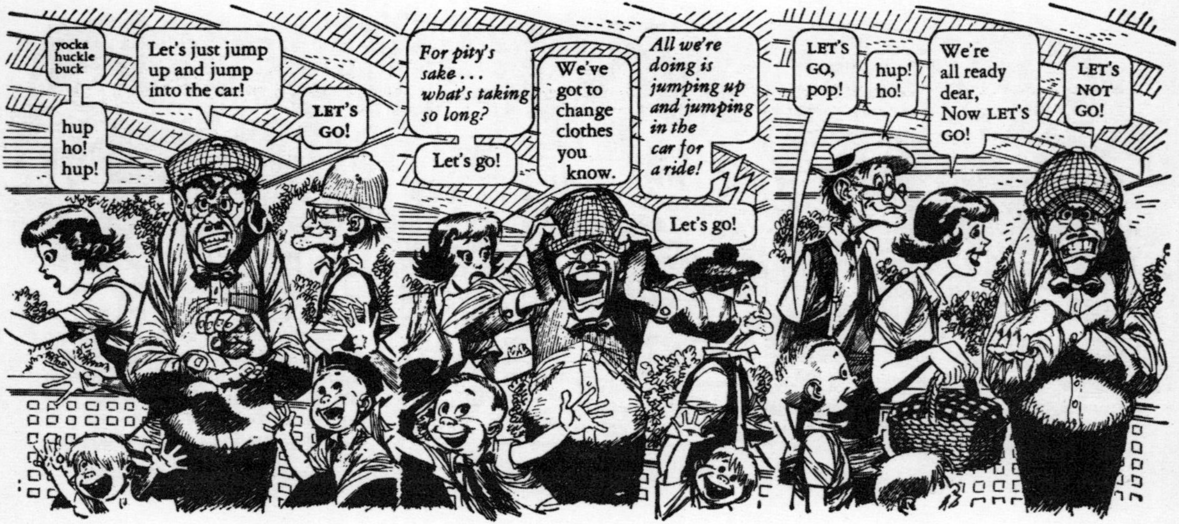
yocka huckle buck
hup ho! hup!
Let's just jump up and jump into the car!
LET'S GO!
For pity's sake . . . what's taking so long?
Let's go!
We've got to change clothes you know.
All we're doing is jumping up and jumping in the car for a ride!
Let's go!
LET'S GO, pop!
hup! ho!
We're all ready dear, Now LET'S GO!
LET'S NOT GO!

Now, say that you are in a car traveling on the turnpike towards the city ... here's the sight you might see ...

In the lane going the opposite way, the traffic is jammed up ... back along the turnpike ... back up the mountain side,

zigzagging down the other side of the mountain then snaking out across the valley ... back up and over the bridge.

. . thence, backed all the way to the city line . . . following a line all along the river . . . over the Riverside drive,

. . . past the suburbs and finally up to a little parkway entrance which marks the tail of the huge line of cars : . .

. . . at the ending of which comes the family finally just beginning to go for a ride and Pop says as follows:

Ha!

Don't worry. It's probably just a little tie-up a few feet ahead.

THE TENSION MOUNTS. The motor, cool and purring an hour ago is hot and choking. The faces once happy and laughing are now sneering, softly muttering oaths. The only thing that keeps the spirit strong to keep moving onward . . . onward, besides the promise of a gas station rest room up ahead, is the vision of a picnic spot like we picture here.

Now about this vision:

Always you see in pictures and movies this here vision of a picnic spot. Always you see a table-cloth spread under a nice shade-tree on a rolling hill in the country with the grass mowed.

So the minute you go on a picnic, you go looking for this type spot. You go looking. And you know what happens?

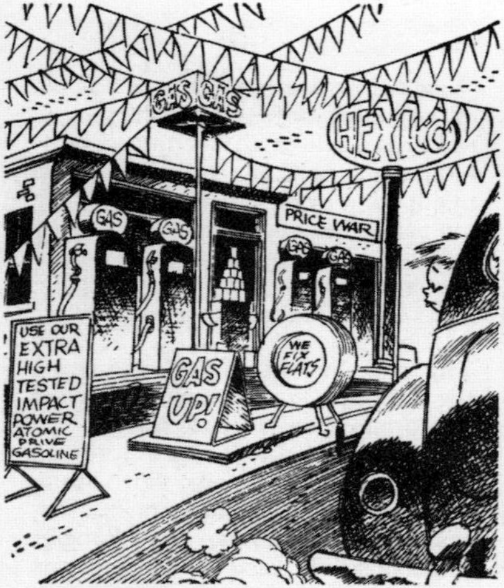
GAS GAS
HEXICO
GAS
GAS
PRICE WAR
USE OUR EXTRA HIGH TESTED IMPACT POWER ATOMIC DRIVE GASOLINE
GAS UP!
WE FIX FLATS

You know what visions you find? Filling stations with trick fluorescent signs that twirl around from the wind.

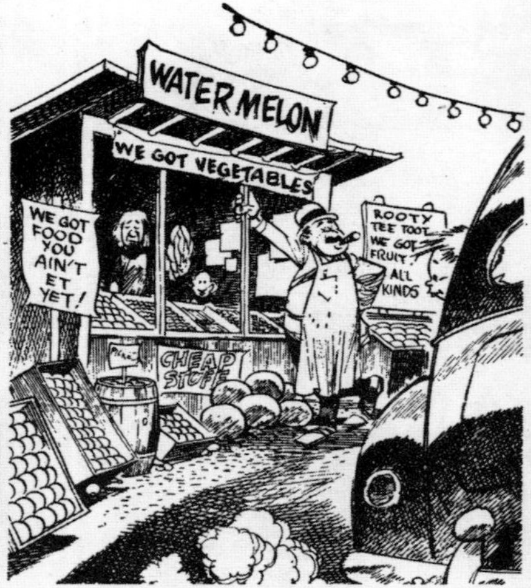
WATER MELON
WE GOT VEGETABLES
WE GOT FOOD YOU AIN'T ET YET!
ROOTY TEE TOOT WE GOT FRUIT ALL KINDS
CHEAP STUFF

You find fruit stands with big special cut-rate bargains right off the farm! (costs just the same in the A and P!)

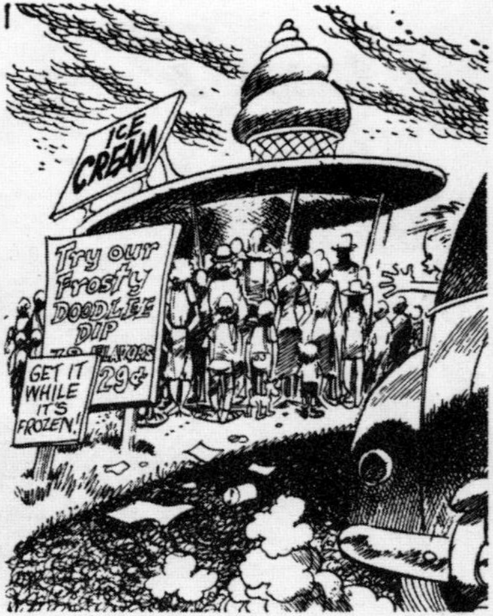
ICE CREAM
Try our Frosty DOODLEE DIP
29¢
GET IT WHILE IT'S FROZEN!

You find Howard Johnson restaurants and those crazy roadside stands with big plaster whipped-cream cones on top.

You find buildings buildings buildings, motels, shopping centers, developments, housing projects, and . . . skyscrapers.

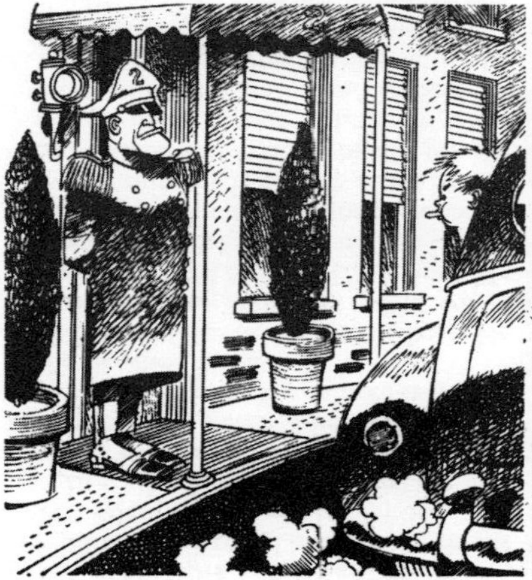

Aha! You find some country between a couple bill-boards. Thick, impenetrable secondary growth full of poison ivy . . . .

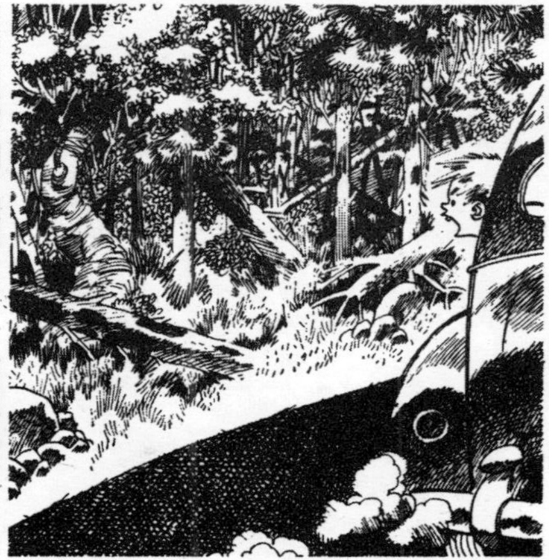

Oho! You suddenly find *exactly* the vision of the picnic spot, surrounded with barbed wire and keep out signs.

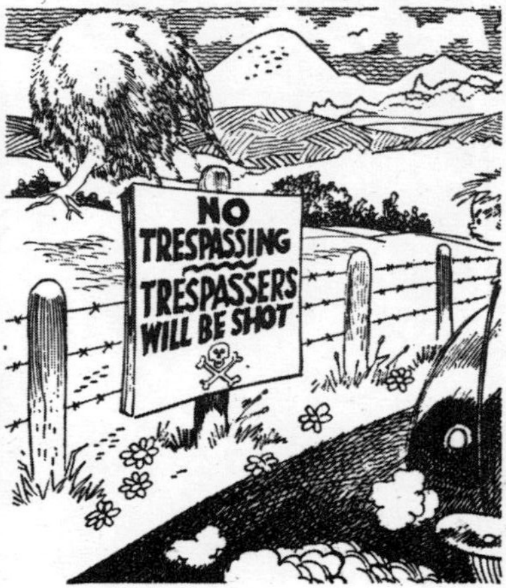
NO TRESPASSING
TRESPASSERS WILL BE SHOT

THE SITUATION DEGENERATES rapidly.

Mom gets excited because she thinks Pop doesn't know where they are.

In the back seat the children are giggling worse and worse. Although now they're hitting each other with the car pillow, you know in a minute it will be the clenched fist.

But, by George, Pop is the boss. He isn't going to take any orders which way to go from Mom or Uncle Fred. He doesn't need help from them.

He asks a policeman for directions.

Ten minutes later they arrive at this beautifully kept public picnic ground nestled in the woods with picnic tables under the trees and their surprise at what they see is clearly mirrored in the wonderous expressions on their faces.

CONTINUED ON NEXT PAGE

And what we see is on the next page!

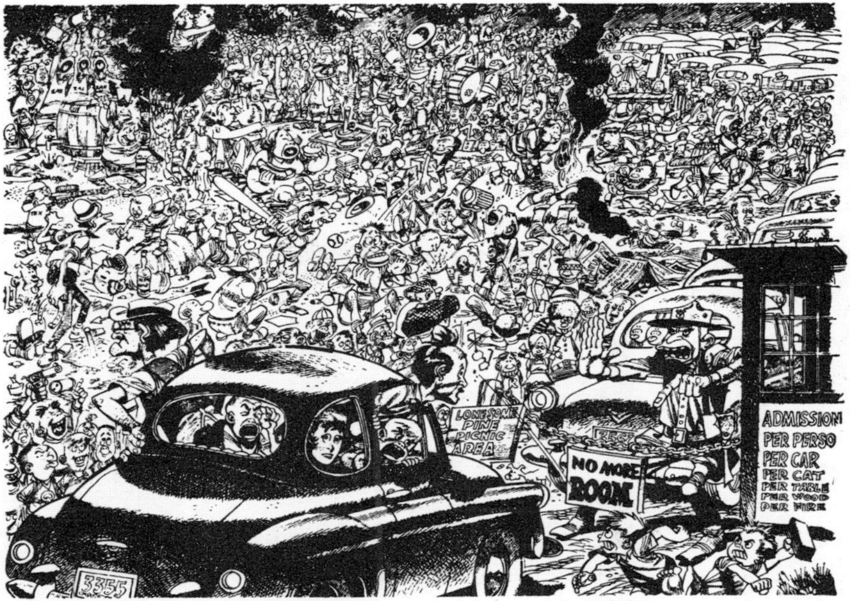
LONESOME PINE PICNIC AREA
NO MORE ROOM
ADMISSION
PER PERSO
PER CAR
PER CAT
PER TABLE
PER WOOD
PER FIRE
3355

A BEAUTIFULLY KEPT PUBLIC PICNIC GROUND NESTLED IN THE WOODS WITH PICNIC TABLES AND FIRE PLACES UNDER THE TREES.

UNFORTUNATELY the beautifully kept public picnic ground is full of people.

So you wearily climb back into your travelling snake-pit and head once more for the open road.

But don't feel too badly. The story has a happy ending.

Eventually the family finds a place to have their picnic with privacy and comforts and all the conveniences. And no trouble getting to either.

Which all goes to show that some of the best things in life are like a moustache and you sometimes overlook them even though they might be under your nose.

And as Uncle Fred snatches the last peanut butter sandwich, and as Pop leans back for a snooze, everybody agrees that here's where they should have had their picnic in the first place.

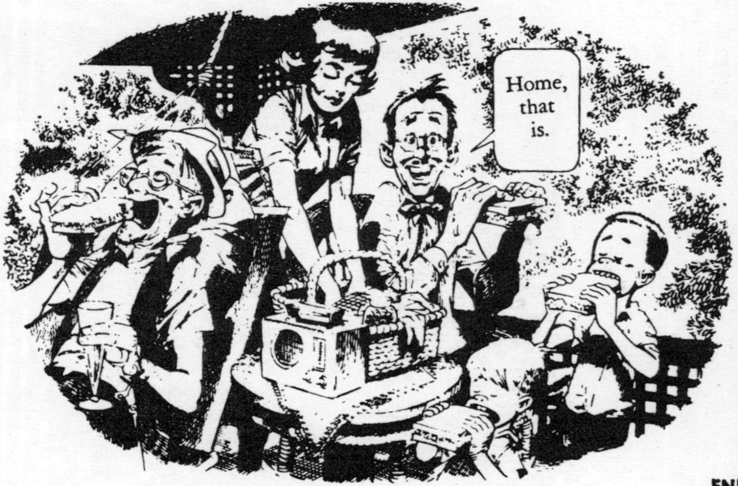
Home, that is.

END

IF YOU SUFFER PAIN

of

HEADACHE NEURITIS NEURALGIA

get

FAST RELIEF

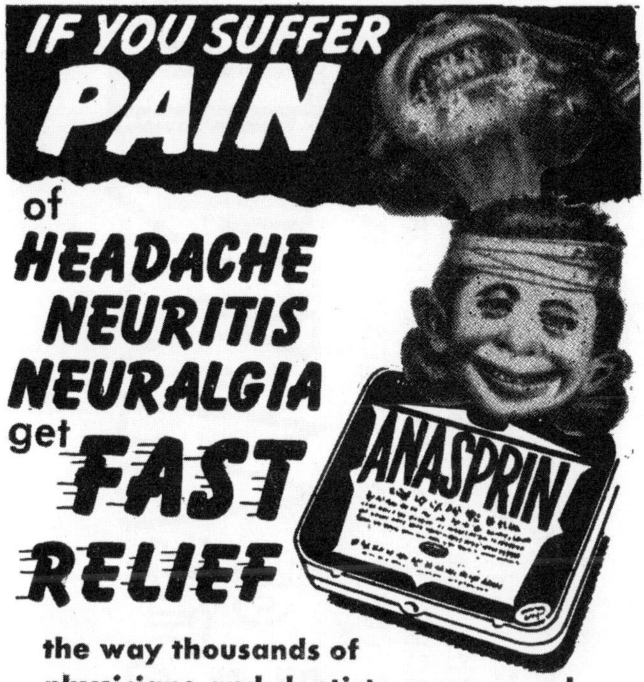
ANASPRIN

the way thousands of physicians and dentists recommend.

HERE'S WHY . Anasprin is like a doctor's prescription. That is, Anasprin contains not just one but a combination of medically proven ingredients . . . and by George, if you had to read the advertisement *this* far, take something for your memory too 'cause we've told this message so many times, you should know it by heart.

TALES FROM THE NORTHWEST DEPT.: THE ROYAL CANADIAN MOUNTIES HAVE HAD MANY A SHINING HERO . . . **RENFREW** OF THE MOUNTIES, **KING** OF THE MOUNTIES, **SILVER EAGLE** OF THE MOUNTIES . . . AND MANY MORE! BUT HERE IS A STORY ON THE **MOST FAMOUS OF THEM ALL!** YES . . . YOU GUESSED IT . . .

MILTIE OF THE MOUNTIES!

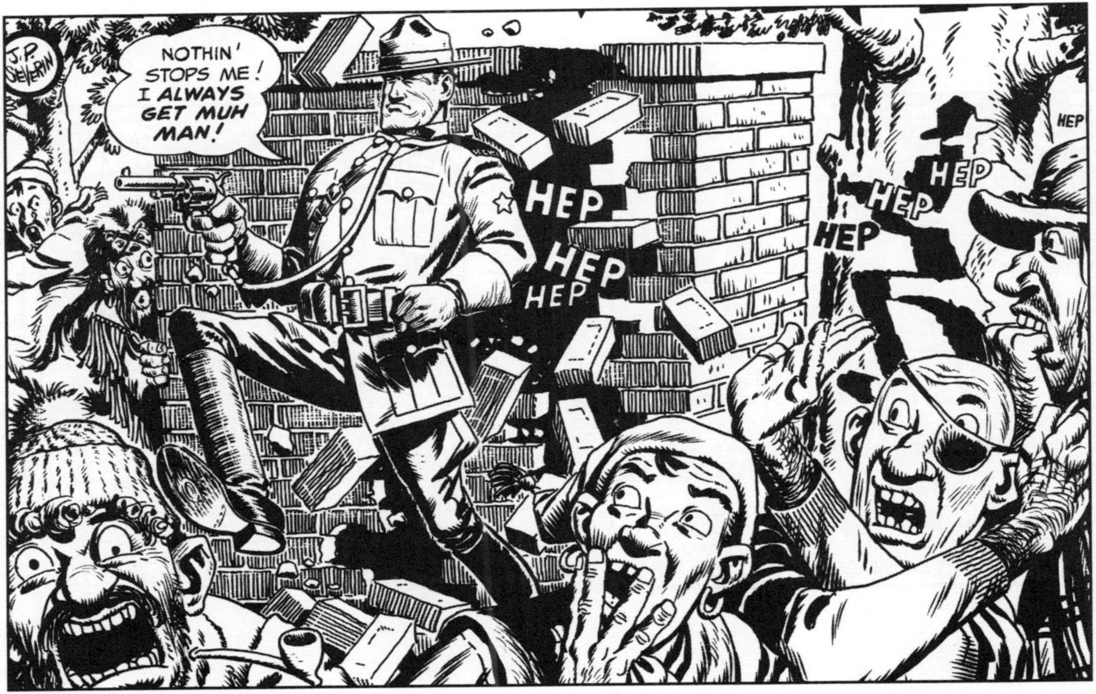
J.P. SEVERIN
NOTHIN' STOPS ME! I ALWAYS GET MUH MAN!
HEP
HEP
HEP
HEP
HEP
HEP
HEP
HEP

OUR STORY STARTS IN A LOG CABIN OFFICE BUILDING IN THE UPPER MANITOBA SWAMPLANDS! SEATED BEHIND A LOG CABIN DESK, SITS SCOTT YARDLAND, **CHIEF** OF THE ROYAL MOUNTIES!
REWARD £20 NANUK THE SCHNOOK
WANTED JERRY DEE NO REWARD
JEB THE REB
WANTED A GOOD FIVE PENCE CIGAR
NOK NOK NOK!
WANTED MIAMI MIKE
WANTED YELLER JAWNDICE
DIRTY ALF
REWARD £500 COLIN DAWKINS
COME IN, NORTHWEST MOUNTIE, AND SHUT THE DOOR!
I SEE WE'RE HAVING A MILD DAY OUT! THANK HEAVEN WE AREN'T HAVING A **REAL STRONG** CANADIAN MOUNTIE TYPE SNOWSTORM!
FROOSH!
1

JACKIE THE MOUNTIE REPORTING, SIR! I GOT MY MAN!
US MOUNTIES ALWAYS GET OUR MAN! THROW HIM IN THE BRIG AND REPORT FOR YOUR NEXT ASSIGNMENT.
WANTED JACK MACDONALD
WANTED
NOK! NOK!
WANTED JACK FOGARTY
REWA £350 JACK FORREST
COME IN, NORTHWEST MOUNTIE!
PHEW! IT SURE IS WARM! US CANADIAN MOUNTIES ARE ONLY USED TO WORKING IN A REAL SNOWSTORM!
FROOOSH!

HERBIE THE MOUNTIE REPORTING, SIR! I GOT MY MAN!
US MOUNTIES ALWAYS GET OUR MAN! THROW HIM IN THE CABOOSE AND REPORT FOR YOUR NEXT ASSIGNMENT!
WANTED JACK DAVIS
NOK! NOK!
WANTED JACK BRESLIN
REWARD £50 JACK KAMEN
COME IN, NORTHWEST MOUNTIE!
HERE COMES ANOTHER ONE OF MY MOUNTIES! MAKE ROOM FOR ANOTHER PRISONER IN THE CABOOSE!
FROOOOSH!!

JERKIE THE MOUNTIE REPORTING, SIR!... I DIDN'T GET MY MAN!
I TRAILED HIM FROM HERE TO THE NORTH POLE, ACROSS THE SPITZ-BERGEN GLACIER, OVER THE ARCTIC SEA, AND BACK HERE! I THOUGHT WHILE I WAS PASSING BY I MIGHT WARM MY HANDS!
WANTED CHARLESTON GEORGE
JACK CRAIG
NO WARMING HANDS, NO CHOW, NO NOTHING TILL YOU GET OUT THERE AND GET YOUR MAN!
A DISGRACE TO THE FORCE!

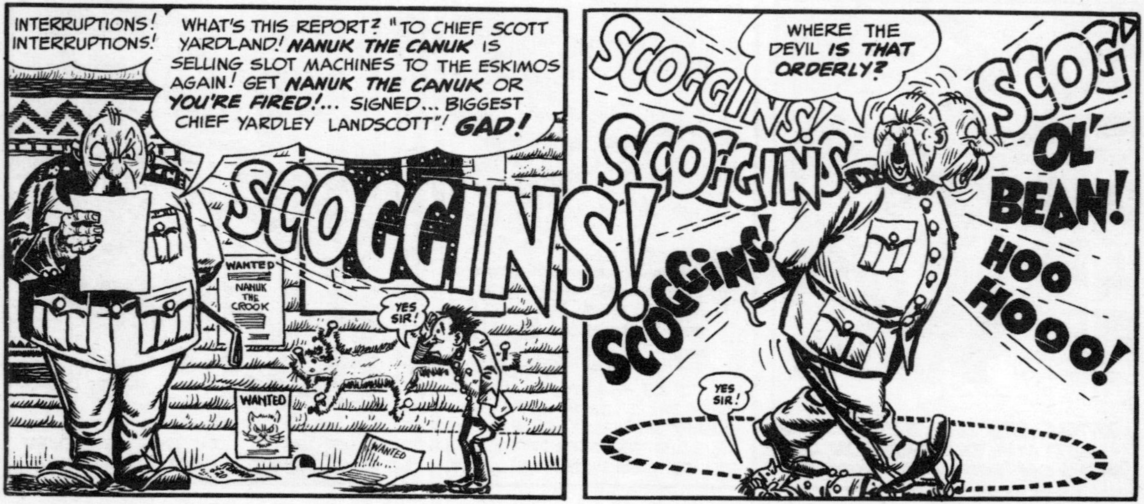
INTERRUPTIONS! INTERRUPTIONS!
WHAT'S THIS REPORT? "TO CHIEF SCOTT YARDLAND! **NANUK THE CANUK** IS SELLING SLOT MACHINES TO THE ESKIMOS AGAIN! GET **NANUK THE CANUK** OR **YOU'RE FIRED!**... SIGNED... BIGGEST CHIEF YARDLEY LANDSCOTT"! **GAD!**
WANTED NANUK THE CROOK
WANTED
WANTED
SCOGGINS!
YES SIR!
SCOGGINS! SCOGGINS
WHERE THE DEVIL **IS THAT ORDERLY?**
SCOG
OL' BEAN!
HOO HOOOO!
SCOGGINS! SCOGGINS!
YES SIR!

AH, THERE YOU ARE, SCOGGINS! WHERE THE DEVIL WERE YOU WHEN I CALLED? ALL RIGHT, MAN! ***UP!... UP***, I SAY!
YES SIR!
GENUINE BISON
SCOGGINS! I'VE GOT A BIT OF A PROBLEM! I'VE GOT TO ROUND UP ***NANUK THE CANUK***, AND I CAN'T THINK OF THE MOUNTIE WHO'S UP TO THE JOB?... WHO CAN I CHOOSE? JACKIE?... HERBIE?
WHAT ABOUT MILTIE THE MOUNTIE, SIR?
A MOUNTIE ALWAYS GETS HIS MAN
EDDY?... TEDDY?... FREDDY?... LENNY?...BENNY?... KENNY?... ERNIE?...BERNIE?... THROKMORTON?... ***THROKMORTON?*** HOW'D HE GET IN HERE?... WILLIE?... PHILLIE?... TILLIE?...
HOW ABOUT MILTIE THE MOUNTIE, SIR?
THIS IS A MAN!

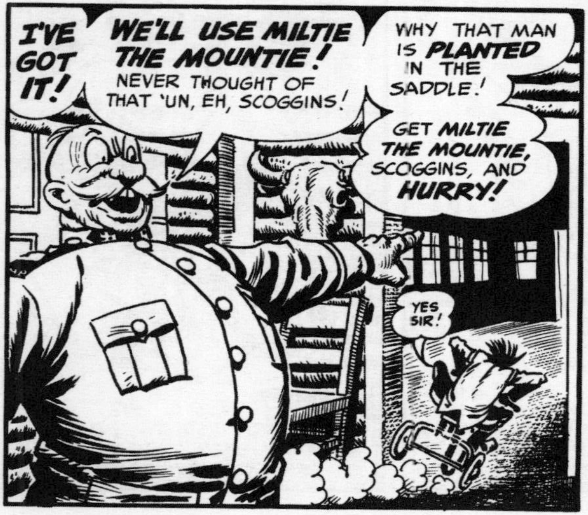
I'VE GOT IT!
WE'LL USE MILTIE THE MOUNTIE! NEVER THOUGHT OF THAT 'UN, EH, SCOGGINS!
WHY THAT MAN IS PLANTED IN THE SADDLE!
GET MILTIE THE MOUNTIE, SCOGGINS, AND HURRY!
YES SIR!

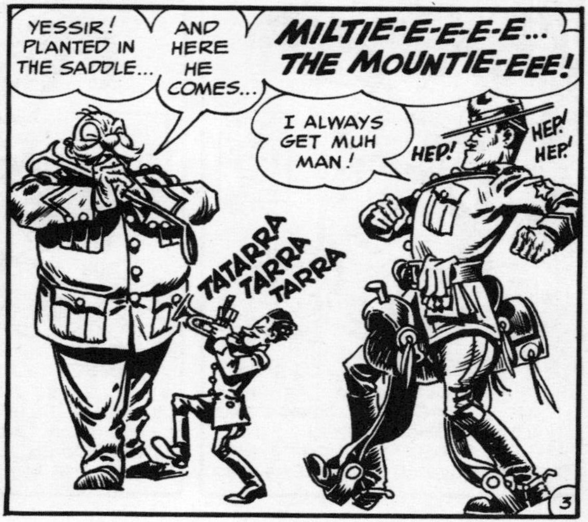
YESSIR! PLANTED IN THE SADDLE...
AND HERE HE COMES...
MILTIE-E-E-E-E... THE MOUNTIE-EEE!
I ALWAYS GET MUH MAN!
HEP! HEP! HEP!
TATARRA TARRA TARRA
3

HAH! SO THAT'S WHERE I LEFT MUH CHEWING GUM!
WELL, CHIEF! I GUESS YOU'VE GOT ANOTHER DIFFICULT ASSIGNMENT FOR ME! BUT DON'T WORRY! I ALWAYS GET MUH MAN!
GOOD BOY, MILTIE! I WANT YOU TO GO OUT THAT DOOR... AND I WANT YOU TO GET NANUK THE CANUK!
NANUK THE CANUK? LIKE I SAID I ALWAYS LIKE A TAN! SO LONG, CHIEF! I WAS JUST ON MY WAY TO FLORIDA!
MILTIE BWAH! MILTIE! DON'T TELL YOUR OLD CHIEFIE YOU'RE AFRAID TO GO OUT THAT DOOR!

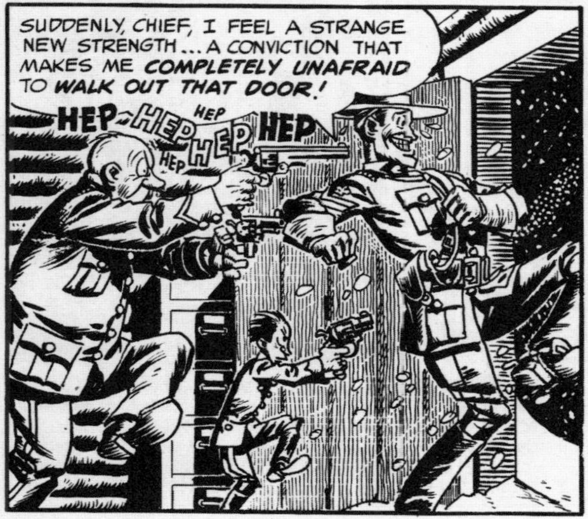
SUDDENLY, CHIEF, I FEEL A STRANGE NEW STRENGTH... A CONVICTION THAT MAKES ME COMPLETELY UNAFRAID TO WALK OUT THAT DOOR!
HEP HEP HEP HEP HEP HEP HEP

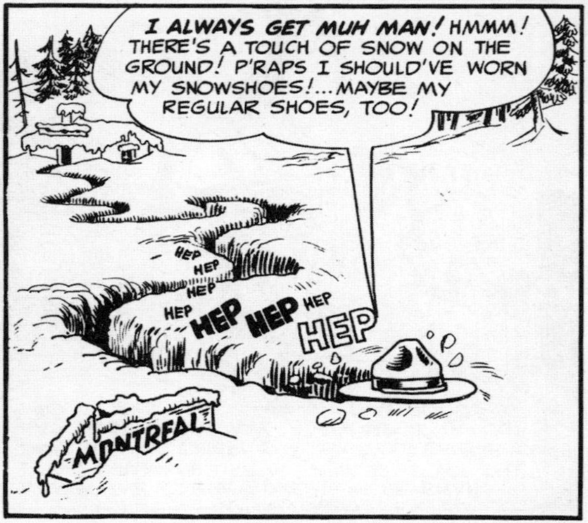
I ALWAYS GET MUH MAN! HMMM! THERE'S A TOUCH OF SNOW ON THE GROUND! P'RAPS I SHOULD'VE WORN MY SNOWSHOES!... MAYBE MY REGULAR SHOES, TOO!
HEP HEP HEP HEP HEP HEP HEP HEP
MONTREAL

NOW TO FIND NANUK THE KANUK'S TRAIL! HAH! FOOTPRINTS IN THE SNOW! CARIBOU? BEAR? COW? WAIT! IT SAYS 'GOODYEAR RUBBER' ON THESE FOOTPRINTS! THEY MUST BE A MAN'S!
HEP HEP HEP
I WILL FOLLOW TRAIL!
HAH! HERE... ANOTHER SET OF PRINTS JOINS THE FIRST! IF THIS IS NANUK, HE HAS A PARTNER!
HEP HEP HEP HEP
HAH! HERE... ANOTHER SET OF PRINTS JOIN! IF THIS IS NANUK, HE MUST HAVE TWO PARTNERS!
HEP HEP HEP HEP
4

HAH! THE TRAIL IS JOINED BY ANOTHER SET OF PRINTS! AND ANOTHER AND ANOTHER AND ANOTHER AND ANOTHER ANU ANUTHEU....
WOW! NANUK HAS A WHOLE ARMY!
PHOOEY! SO MANY FOOT-PRINTS, I LOST THE WHOLE TRAIL!
HEY, FELLA? ...YOU SEE THIS HERE NANUK THE CANUK?
YEAH! I'M NANUK THE CANUK! I DECIDED TO BRING MYSELF IN FOR THE REWARD MONEY!
WANTED
NANUK THE CANUK
£5000 REWARD
HEP HEP HEP

... YOU CRAZY, BOY? THE MAN DON'T GET HIS MAN! THE MOUNTIE GETS HIS MAN!
YOU'LL NEVER GET ME, MOUNTIE!
I, MILTIE THE MOUNTIE, ALWAYS GET MUH MAN!
I'LL FOLLOW YOU...THROUGH THE RAIN...
HEP HEP.. HEP
...THROUGH THE SLEET...
HEP HEP HEP

...THROUGH THE SNOW AND HAIL...
HEP HEP HEP
...THE MAILS MUST GET THROUGH!
HEY, WAIT A MINUTE!...I'M NOT A MAILMAN!
...I'M MILTIE THE MOUNTIE, AND I'M CHASING NANUK THE CANUK! HE'S TRAPPED IN A DEAD END AHEAD! I TOLD YOU I ALWAYS GET MUH MAN!
DEAD END
5

NANUK THE CANUK! YOU'RE UP AGAINST A DEAD END AND WHEN I GET THROUGH, THE REST OF YOU WILL BE DEAD TOO!
DEAD END
WAIT, MILTIE!
BEFORE YOU SHOOT, LET ME OPEN UP MY COAT! I JUST STOLE IT BRAND-NEW AND I'D HATE TO GET ANY NASTY OLD BULLET HOLES IN IT!
DEAD END

O.K. NOW, MILTIE! GO AHEAD AND SHOOT! GO AHEAD! IT'S EASY!
FLAP!
SHOOT! SHOOT! HERE, I'LL SHOW YOU HOW! SEE? YOU HOLD THE GUN ...
...WITH YOUR FINGER ON THE TRIGGER... FRONT OF GUN POINTING TO HE WHO IS TO BE SHOT!
THEN YOU SIMPLY APPLY PRESSURE ON TRIGGER ONCE... TWICE... THRICE... FICE... AS MANY TIMES AS NECESSARY!
BAM!
BAM!
BAM!
BAM!
BAM!
BAM!

UGH!...I AM MILTIE THE MOUNTIE! I...I ALWAYS G-GET MUH M-M-M-MAN!
UNFORTUNATELY THIS SHALL NOT HOLD TRUE FOR NANUK THE CANUK!... FOR YOU SEE... NANUK THE CAKUK...
... IS A W-W-WOMAN!
6

POETRY DEPT.: TODAY WE DO DISCUSS . . . IN MANNER MARKED OF US . . . (OF WRECKING AND WRACKING, AND COMICAL BOOK HACKING) . . . THE POEM 'HESPERUS'! . . . AND SO PRESENTING THUS . . . WITH WORDS UNCHANGED OF CUSS . . . FROM GOOD TO WORSE, THE 'HESPERUS' VERSE TO THE . . .

WRECK OF THE HESPERUS

by H.W. LONGFELLOW

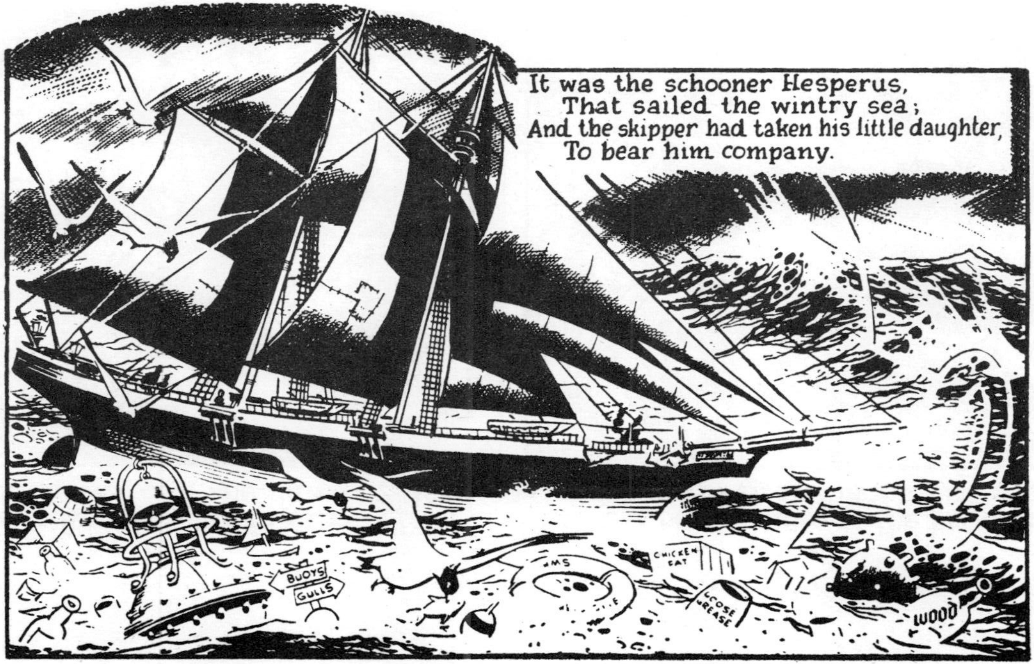
It was the schooner Hesperus,
That sailed the wintry sea;
And the skipper had taken his little daughter,
To bear him company.
BUOYS
GULLS
CHICKEN FAT
LOOSE GREASE
WOOD

Blue were her eyes as the fairy-flax,
Her cheeks like the dawn of day,

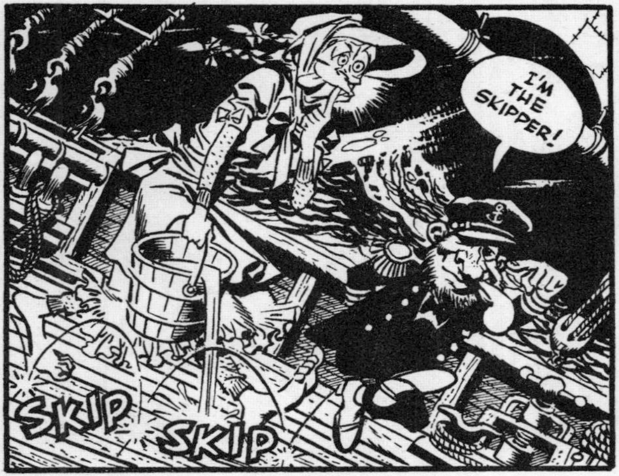
I'M THE SKIPPER!
SKIP
SKIP

And her bosom white as the hawthorn buds,
That ope in the month of May.

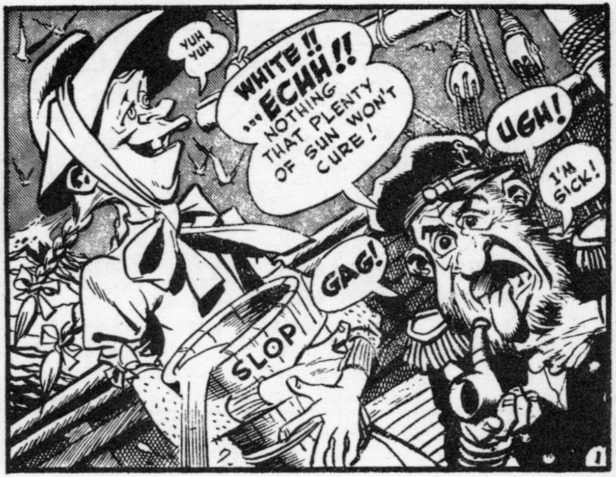
YUH YUH
WHITE!! ...ECHH!! NOTHING THAT PLENTY OF SUN WON'T CURE!
UGH!
I'M SICK!
GAG!
SLOP

The skipper he stood beside the helm,
His pipe was in his mouth;

And he watched the veering flaw did blow
The smoke now west, now south.

WAIT! WAIT! YOU GOT TO SPILL THAT SLOP WITH THE VEERING FLAW!
HEAVE HO!
WAIT! WAIT! YES! THE VEERING FLAW! ... NOW WEST!
YUH YUH
WAIT! WAIT! THE VEERING FLAW! ... NOW SOUTH!
SLOP!

Then up spake an old sailor,
Had sailed the Spanish Main:

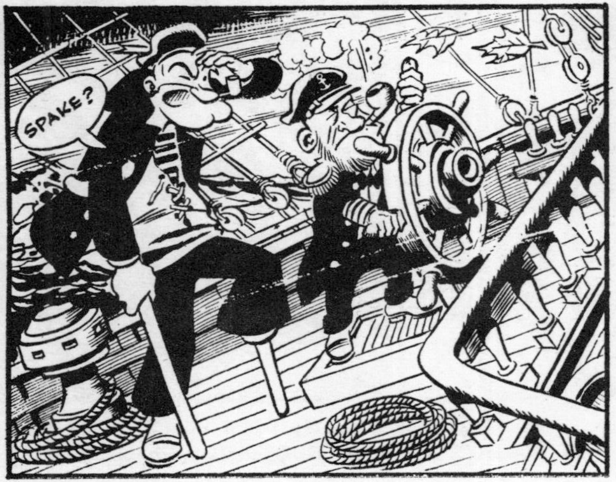
SPAKE?

"I pray thee, put into yonder port,
For I fear a hurricane."

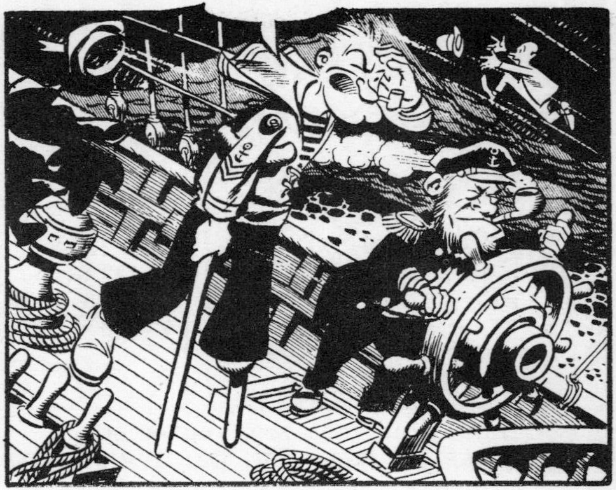

"Last night the moon had a golden ring,
And tonight no moon we see!"

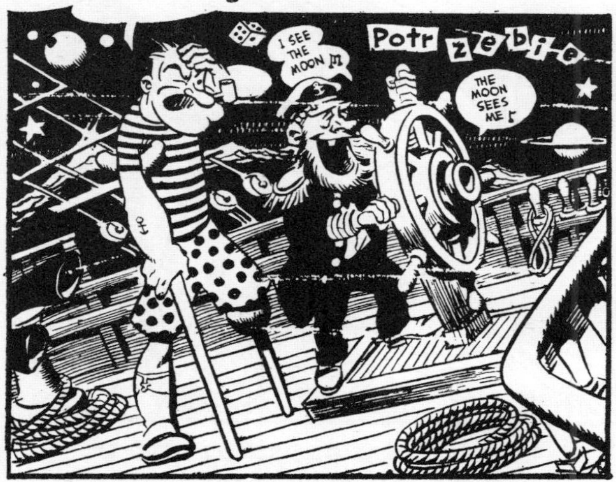
I SEE THE MOON
Potrzebie
THE MOON SEES ME

The skipper, he blew a whiff from his pipe,
And a scornful laugh laughed he.

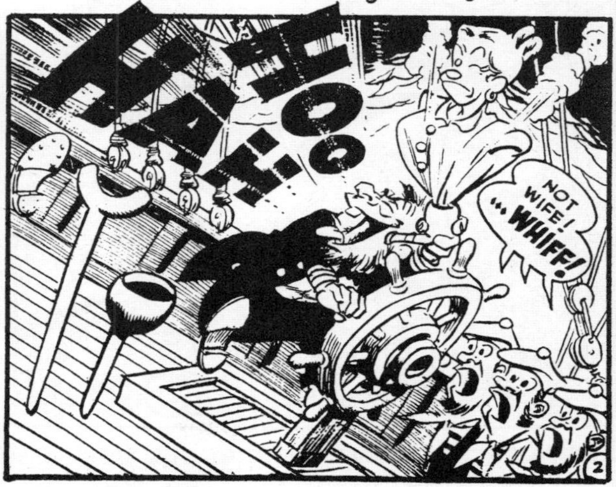
NOT WIFE! ... WHIFF!

Colder and louder blew the wind,
A gale from the north-east;

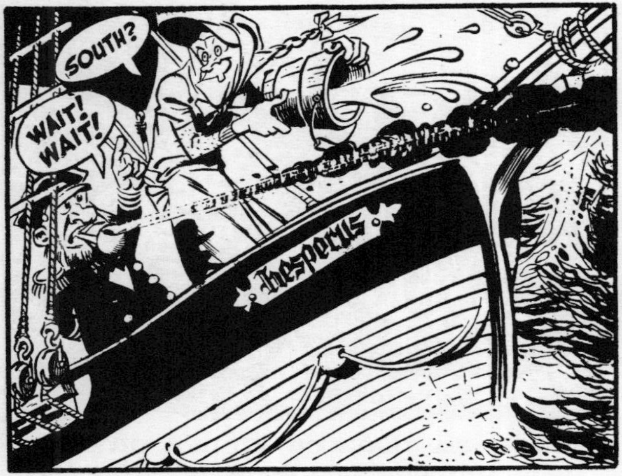
SOUTH?
WAIT! WAIT!
Hesperus

The snow fell hissing in the brine,
And the billows frothed like yeast.

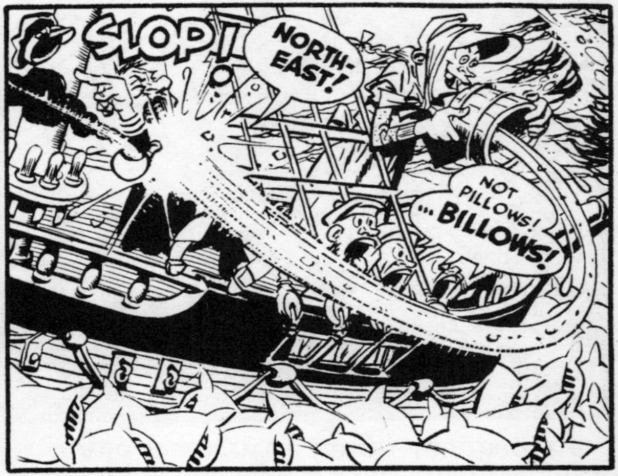
SLOP!
NORTH-EAST!
NOT PILLOWS! ...BILLOWS!

Down came the storm and smote amain
The vessel in its strength;

She shuddered and paused like a frightened steed
Then leaped her cable's length.

NOW LOOK! YOU GOT ME ALL WET!
KTAK
KTAK
BALOWM!
NOT THE DAUGHTER! ... THE HESPERUS!
NOT THE TABLE ... THE CABLE!
PIP

"Come hither! Come hither! My little daughter,
And do not tremble so;"

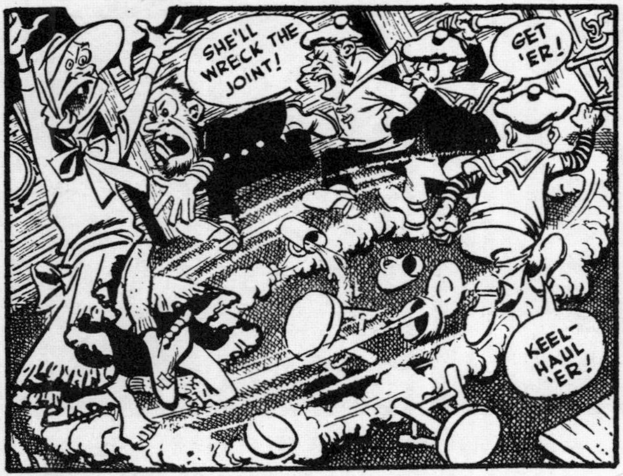
SHE'LL WRECK THE JOINT!
GET 'ER!
KEEL-HAUL 'ER!

"For I can weather the roughest gale,
That ever wind did blow."

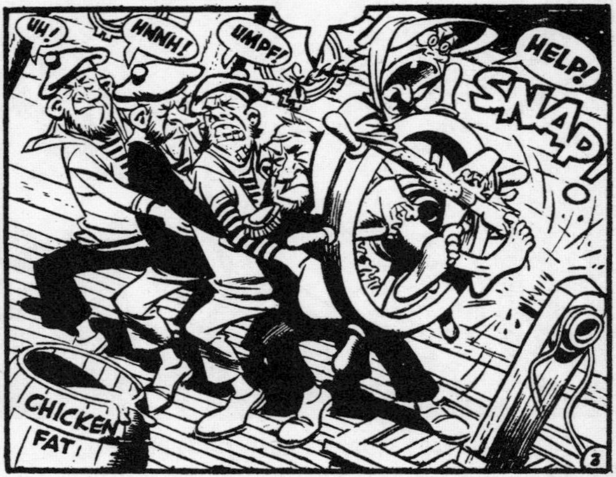
UH!
HNNH!
UMPF!
HELP!
SNAP!
CHICKEN FAT!

He wrapped her warm in his seaman's coat
Against the stinging blast;
He cut a rope from a broken spar,
And bound her to the mast.

WHEW! NOW MAYBE I CAN SAIL THIS FURSHLUGGINER SHIP!
SLAM!

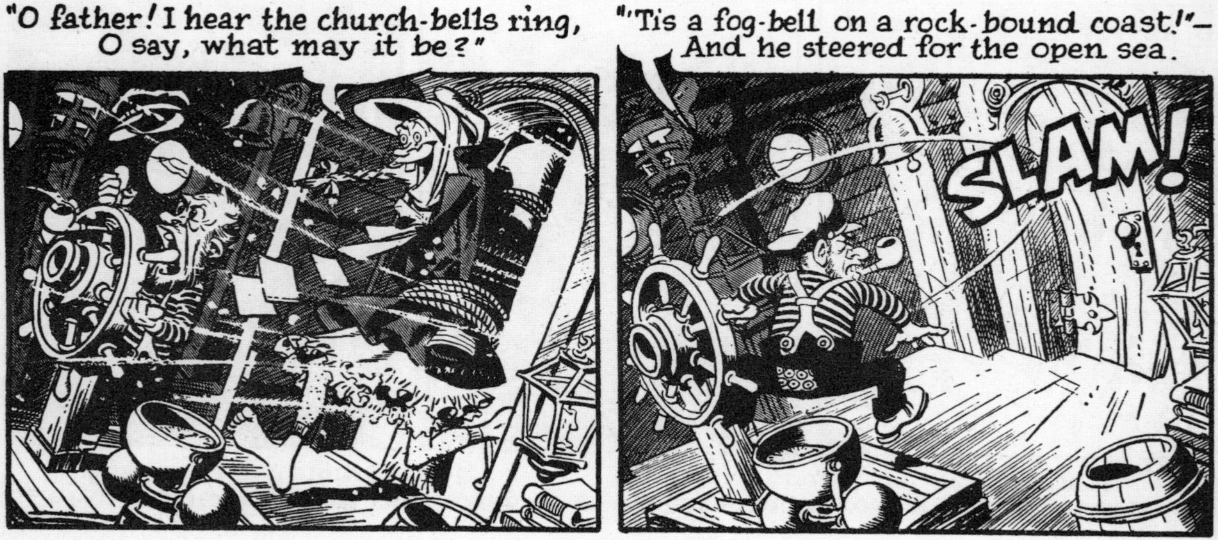
"O father! I hear the church-bells ring, O say, what may it be?"
"'Tis a fog-bell on a rock-bound coast!"— And he steered for the open sea.
SLAM!

"O father! I hear the sound of guns,
    O say, what may it be?

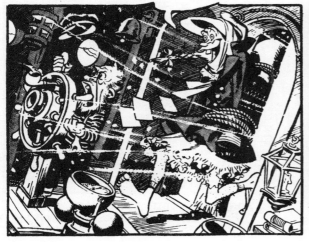

"Some ship in distress, that cannot live
    In such an angry sea!"

SLAM!

"O father! I see a gleaming light,
O say, what may that be?"

But the father answered never a word,
A frozen corpse was he.

Lashed to the helm, all stiff and stark
With his face turned to the skies;

The lantern gleamed through the gleaming snow
On his fixed and glassy eyes...

TINK
AND WHY NOT GLASSY EYES?
CONTACT LENSES!

...And fast through the midnight dark and drear,
Through the whistling sleet and snow,

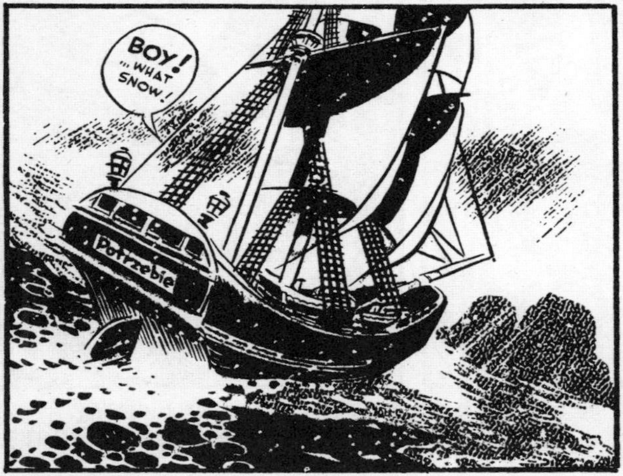
BOY! ...WHAT SNOW!
Potrzebie

Like a sheeted ghost, the vessel swept
Towards the reef of Norman's Woe.

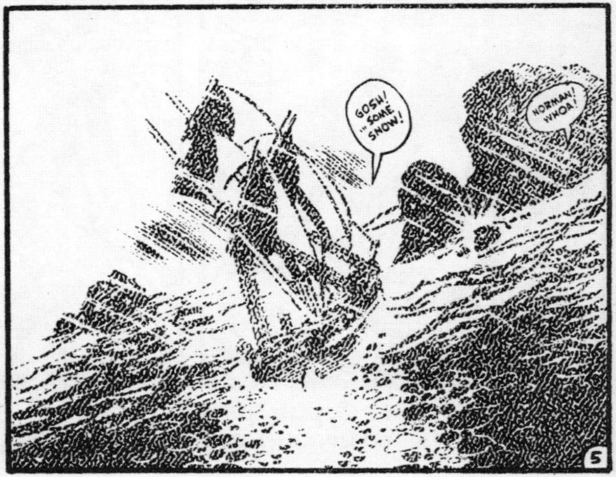
GOSH! ...SOME SNOW!
NORMAN! WHOA!
5

And ever, the fitful gusts between,
A sound came from the land;

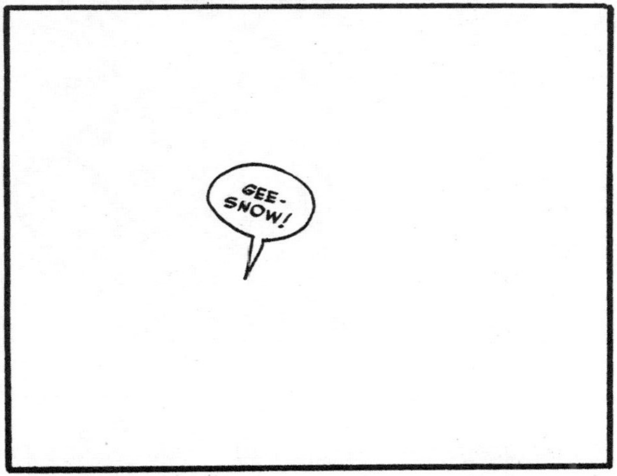
GEE-
SNOW!

It was the sound of the trampling surf,
On the rocks and the hard sea-sand.

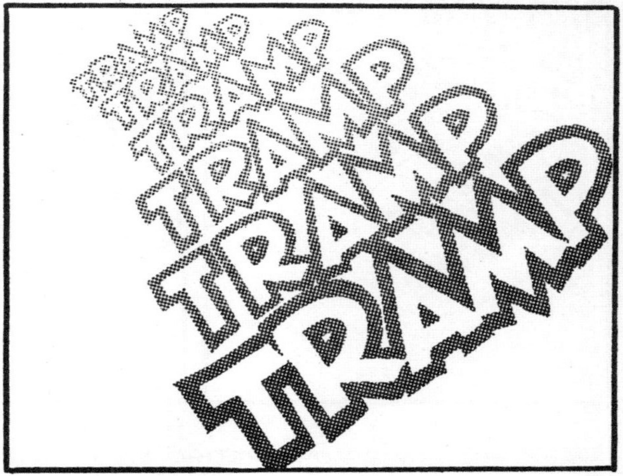
TRAMP
TRAMP
TRAMP
TRAMP
TRAMP
TRAMP
TRAMP

The breakers were right beneath her bows,
She drifted a weary wreck,

And a whooping billow swept the crew
Like icicles from her deck.

BREAK
BREAK
BREAK
BREAK
BREAK
DRIFT
DRIFT
DRIFT
DRIFT
WHOOP
WHOOP
WHOOP
WHOOP
WHOOP
BILLOWS! ...NOT PILLOWS!

She struck where the white and fleecy waves
Looked soft as carded wool,

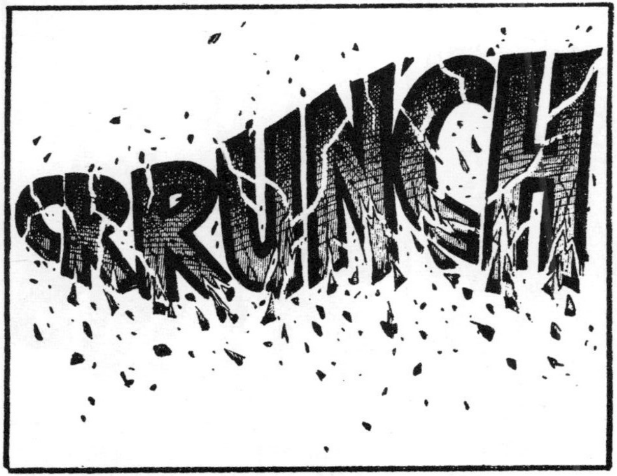
CRUNCH

But the cruel rocks, they gored her side,
Like the horns of an angry bull.

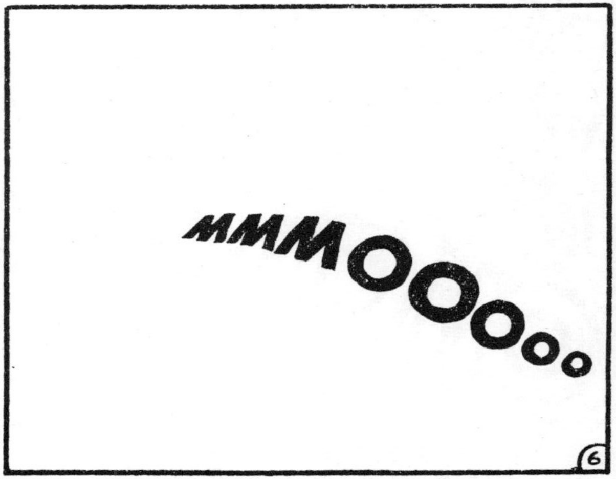
MMMOOOOoo
6

Her rattling shrouds, all sheathed in ice,
With masts, went by the board;
Like a vessel of glass, she stove and sank,
Ho! ho! the breakers roared.

RATTLE
RATTLE
RATTLE
YOU'RE FADED!
CRASH!
TINKLE
TINK
TINKLE
TRINKLE
PLINK
TINK
TINK
KLIK
PLING
HEE
SNARF
HEH
HA
HOOH
YAK
YUK
HA
HO
HUH
HO HO
HYUK
HEE HEE
HOO HOO
HYAW
HAW
HAW
HO
HYEH YEH
YUK
YUK
HEE HA
HOO

At daybreak, on the bleak sea-beach,
A fisherman stood aghast,

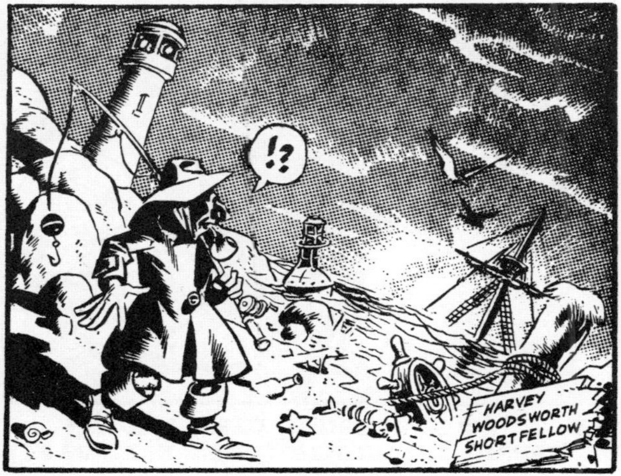
!?
HARVEY WOODSWORTH SHORTFELLOW

To see the form of a maiden fair,
Lashed close to a drifting mast.

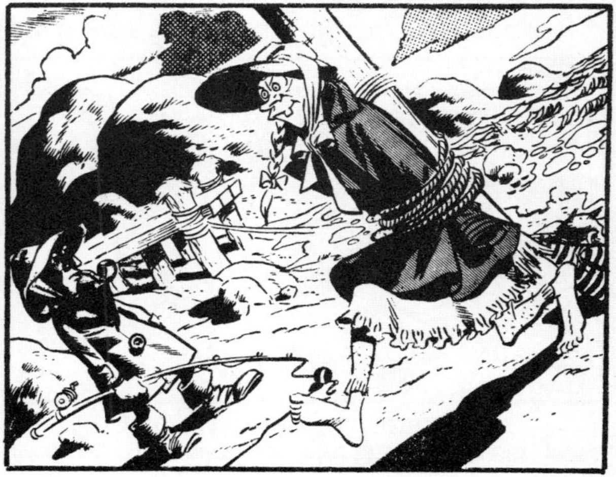

The salt sea was frozen on her breast,
The salt tears in her eyes;

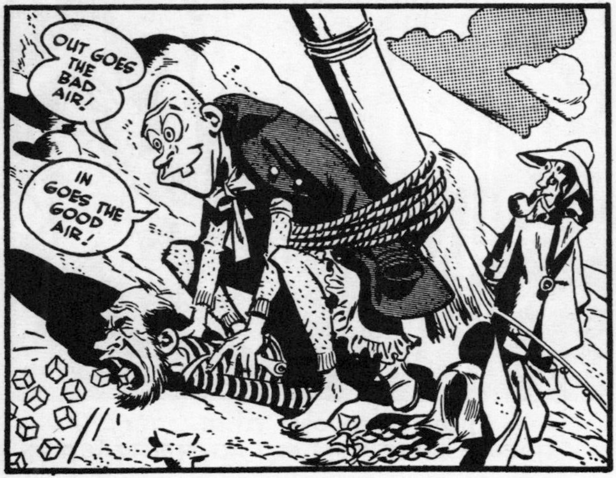
OUT GOES THE BAD AIR!
IN GOES THE GOOD AIR!

And he saw her hair like the brown sea-weed,
On the billows fall and rise.

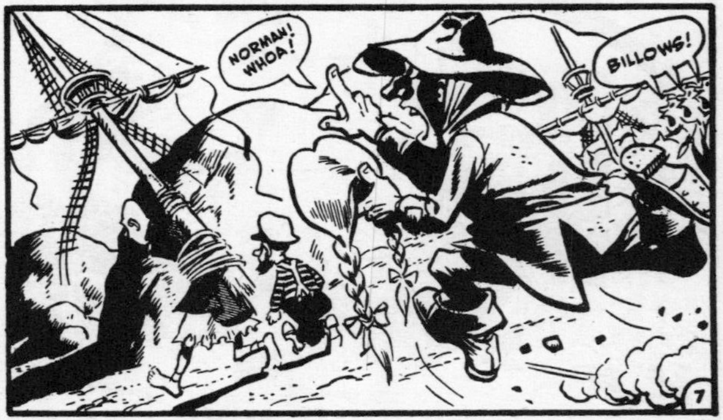
NORMAN! WHOA!
BILLOWS!
7

Such was the wreck of the Hesperus,
In the midnight and the snow.
Christ save us all from a death like this
On the reef of Norman's Woe!

HOLLYWOOD DEPT.: ...NOTICE THE WAY THEY START SOME MOVIES NOWADAYS?... NO TITLE AT THE BEGINNING... THE MOVIE STARTS RIGHT IN WITH A SCENE...

...LIKE IN THIS PICTURE WE SAW THE OTHER MONTH, IT STARTS WITH NO TITLE, NO CREDITS, NO NOTHING! ...JUST A SCENE OF A HIGHWAY STRETCHING WAY OUT...

...NOTHING ELSE!...JUST A HIGHWAY!...THAT'S HOW THE PICTURE STARTS!...FOR A HALF AN HOUR, JUST A HIGHWAY!...BUT YOU KNOW, BY THE WAY THAT HIGHWAY GOES, SOMETHING'S COMING!

...YOU KNOW, BY THE WAY THAT HIGHWAY STRETCHES TO THE HORIZON, SOMETHING'S GOING TO COME DOWN THAT HIGHWAY! ...AND SURE ENOUGH...SOON YOU HEAR A NOISE!

...A FAINT ROAR COMING DOWN THE HIGHWAY! *YOU LOOK TO SEE WHAT'S COMING DOWN THE HIGHWAY! LOUDER AND LOUDER...COMING DOWN THE HIGHWAY!...STILL...NOTHING ON THE HIGHWAY... HEY!*

...*WAIT A MINUTE!*... *YOU GUYS GOT THE WRONG HIGHWAY!*... *TAKE THEM MOTORCYCLES AND GO BACK AND COME UP THE RIGHT HIGHWAY!*

O.K.!... SO HERE WE GO AGAIN! TRYING TO EXPLAIN HOW THIS MOVIE STARTS!... SO HERE'S THIS HIGHWAY AGAIN... NOTHING ON IT!... NOUGHT... ZERO... NONE... NOTHING!

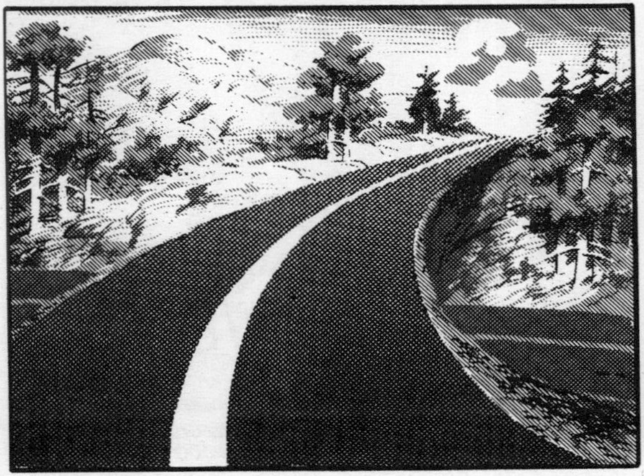

...ALL OF A SUDDEN, YOU HEAR A NOISE... AH, HERE THEY COME... A GROUP OF MOTORCYCLE RIDERS SPEEDING ALONG IN THE DISTANCE... **CLOSER... LOUDER... FASTER...**

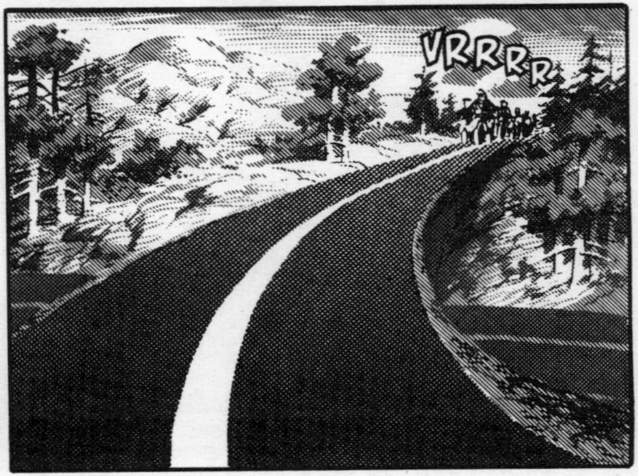
VRRRRR

...THE SPEED BUILDS UP!... SOUND BUILDS UP!... THESE MOTORCYCLES ROAR RIGHT DOWN ON TOP OF YOU... SCARE YOU TO DEATH!... WHAT A SCENE!

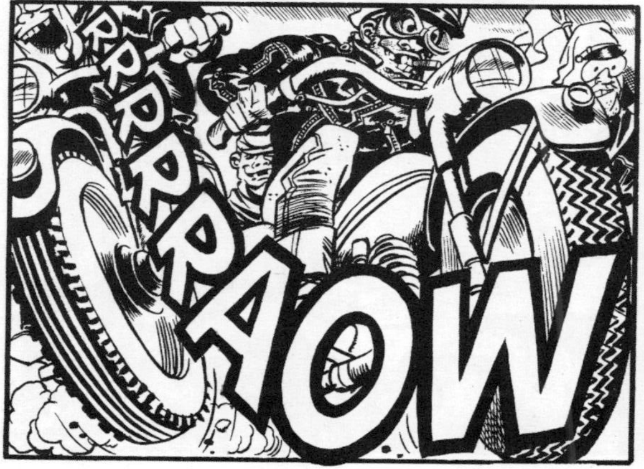
RRRRRAOW

...THEN THE CAMERA PANS ONTO THE LEADER OF THIS BUNCH OF MOTORCYCLE CRAZIES AND HERE'S HOW THEY SNEAK THE TITLE IN... SOMETHING LIKE THIS...

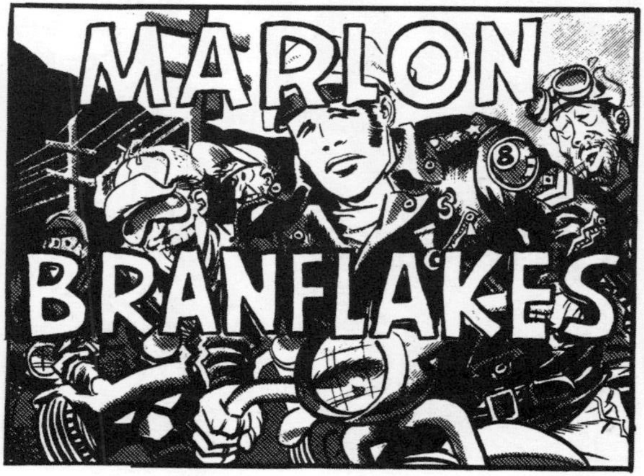
MARLON
BRANFLAKES

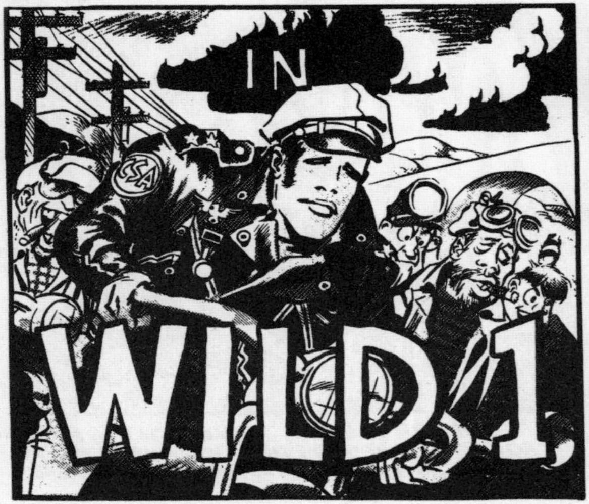
IN
WILD 1

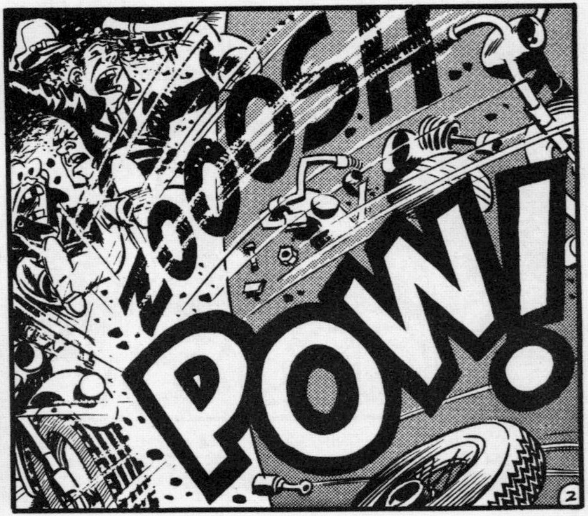
WOOOSH
POW!

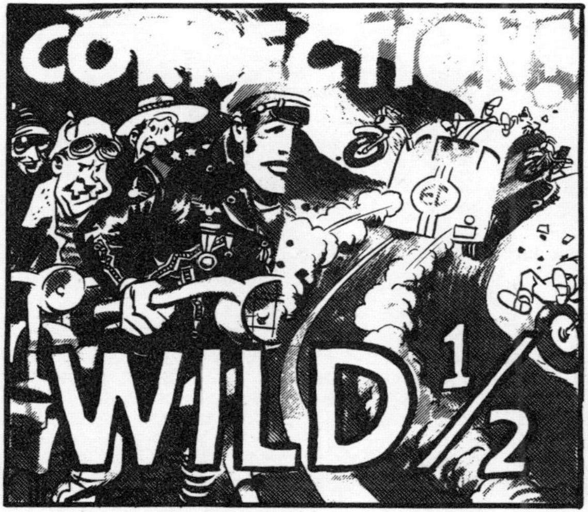
WILD 1/2

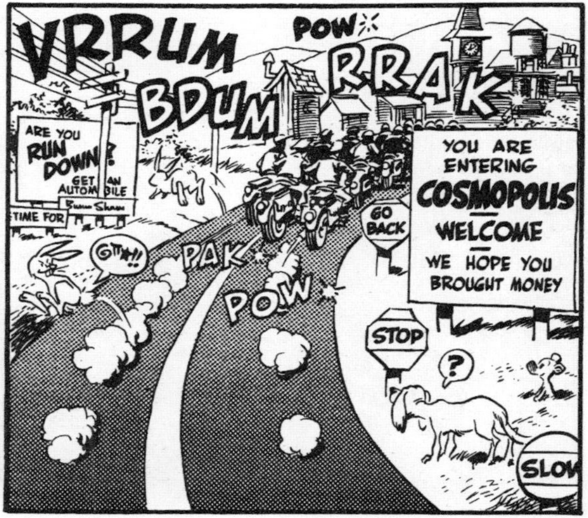
VRRUM
POW
BDUM
RRAK
ARE YOU RUN DOWN?
GET AN AUTOM BILE
TIME FOR
GO BACK
YOU ARE ENTERING COSMOPOLIS
WELCOME
WE HOPE YOU BROUGHT MONEY
PAK
POW
STOP
?
SLOW

AT EASE, YOU KATS!... WE'RE GOIN' TO TAKE OVER THIS TOWN AND REALLY HAVE A BALL!... I MEAN, WE'RE GOIN' TO GO, MAN! ...I MEAN, WE'RE GOIN' TO MAKE THE JOINT JUMP, I MEAN!
WHADZ HE MEAN?
...SAY, NOW LOOKA HERE, YOUNG FELLER! ...YOU'RE WELCOME TO STAY IN THIS TOWN, YOUNG FELLER, AS LONG AS YOU DON'T CAUSE NO TROUBLE!
...I HATE COPS!
B.B.O.P.
PUSH!

DON'T LET HIM GET AWAY WITH THAT!
...YOU'RE THE POLICE OFFICER IN THIS TOWN!
...IF YOU SHOW THEM KIND YOU'RE SCARED, THEY'LL RUN ALL OVER YOU!
GET TOUGH!
RIGHT!
NOW LOOKY HERE, BWAH! I'VE STOOD ENOUGH GUFF FROM YOU!...YOU JUST STEP OUT OF LINE ONCE! I'LL SEND YOU OUT TO A PLACE, YOU CAN'T HEAR THE DOGS BARK! HEAR ME, BWAH? NOW, WHATAYA SAY! NOW, WHATAYA SAY!
GRR GRR GRR
...I HATE COPS!
B.B.O.P.
PUSH!
3

...LIKE I SAID, WE'RE TAKIN' OVER, MAN.!
...I MEAN I WANT A DETAIL TO ROUND UP ALL THE SQUARES OF MILITARY AGE...
...I MEAN I WANT HOSTAGES TAKEN!
...I MEAN...
Potrzebie
SO WHADZ HE MEAN?
UH-OH!... WHEN JOHNNY GETS A LOOK IN HIS EYE LIKE THAT... HE'S LOOKIN' AT WHAT HE LIKES THE BEST...
WOOD
TILT
B.B.O.P.
REBOP

PUSH!
PUSH!
PUSH!
PUSH!

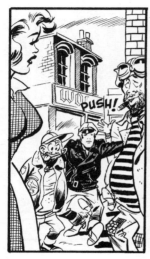

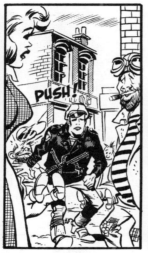

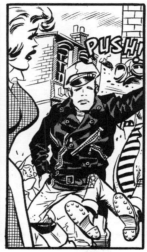

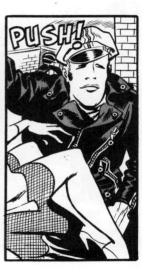

GOSHAROOTIE!
...AND WHAT HE LIKES THE BEST IS ***MOTOR-CYCLES!***
MOTORCYC
SAY, MAN!... DIG MY NEW ***CYKE!*** ... I HADDA GO BROKE TO GET THIS ***CYKE!***
...I HADDA GO BROKE THE STORE WINDOW!
...SAY! ...WHERE'S THE SOLID DOLL THAT WAS STANDING HERE BEFORE?
SHE'S GONE!
...I ***KNOW*** SHE'S GONE, MAN... AND COOL BESIDES!
OTORCYCLES
4

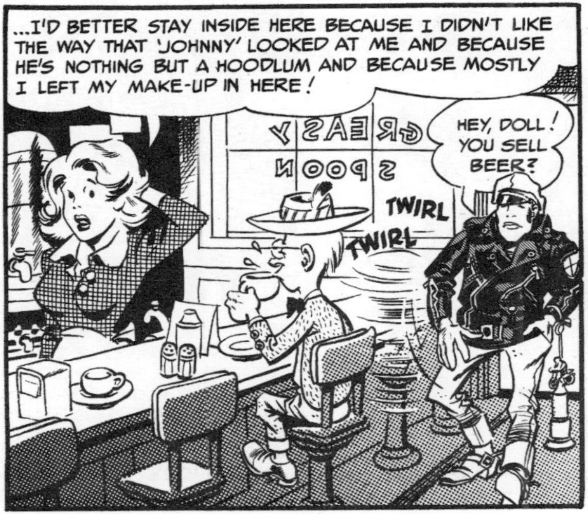
...I'D BETTER STAY INSIDE HERE BECAUSE I DIDN'T LIKE THE WAY THAT 'JOHNNY' LOOKED AT ME AND BECAUSE HE'S NOTHING BUT A HOODLUM AND BECAUSE MOSTLY I LEFT MY MAKE-UP IN HERE!
HEY, DOLL! YOU SELL BEER?
TWIRL
TWIRL

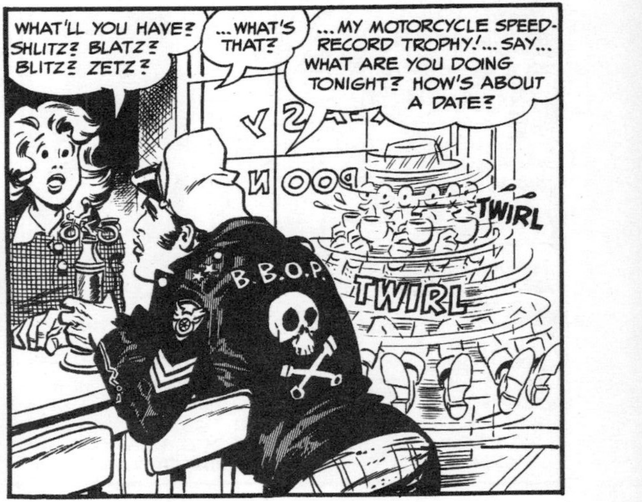
WHAT'LL YOU HAVE? SHLITZ? BLATZ? BLITZ? ZETZ?
...WHAT'S THAT?
...MY MOTORCYCLE SPEED-RECORD TROPHY!... SAY... WHAT ARE YOU DOING TONIGHT? HOW'S ABOUT A DATE?
TWIRL
B.B.O.P.
TWIRL

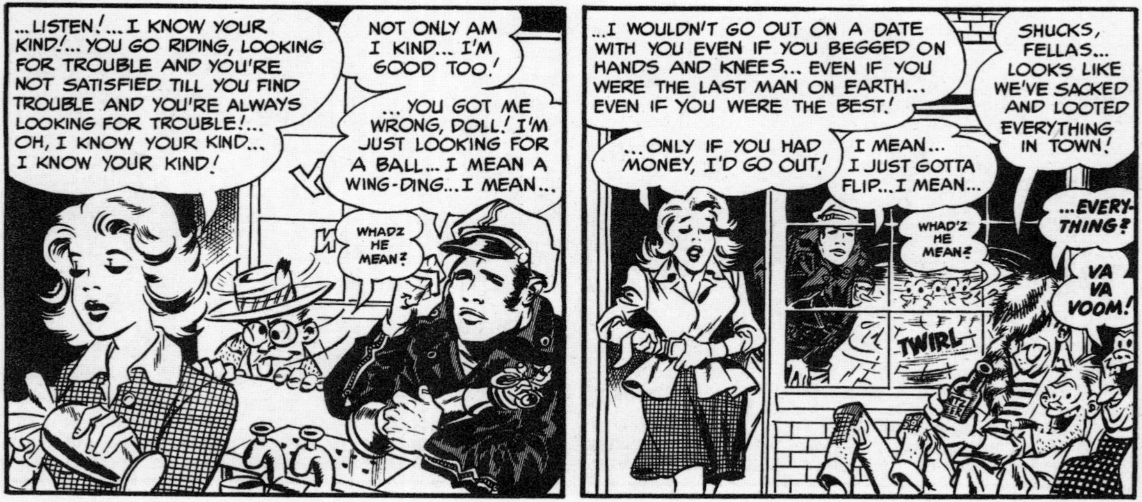
...LISTEN!...I KNOW YOUR KIND!... YOU GO RIDING, LOOKING FOR TROUBLE AND YOU'RE NOT SATISFIED TILL YOU FIND TROUBLE AND YOU'RE ALWAYS LOOKING FOR TROUBLE!... OH, I KNOW YOUR KIND... I KNOW YOUR KIND!
NOT ONLY AM I KIND... I'M GOOD TOO!
... YOU GOT ME WRONG, DOLL! I'M JUST LOOKING FOR A BALL... I MEAN A WING-DING...I MEAN...
WHADZ HE MEAN?
...I WOULDN'T GO OUT ON A DATE WITH YOU EVEN IF YOU BEGGED ON HANDS AND KNEES... EVEN IF YOU WERE THE LAST MAN ON EARTH... EVEN IF YOU WERE THE BEST!
...ONLY IF YOU HAD MONEY, I'D GO OUT!
I MEAN... I JUST GOTTA FLIP...I MEAN...
WHAD'Z HE MEAN?
TWIRL
SHUCKS, FELLAS... LOOKS LIKE WE'VE SACKED AND LOOTED EVERYTHING IN TOWN!
...EVERY-THING?
VA VA VOOM!

POK
POK
POK
SPA
DOW!
TIP TAP TIP TAP
VRUM!
VRUM!
VRUM!
VROOOOW
TIPPITY
TAPPITY
TIPPITY
TAPPITY
WRAMM
TIPPITY
TAP
TIPPITY
TAP
5

KLIP
KLIP
KLIP
KLIP
VRAOW!
KLIP
KLIP
KLIP
KLIP
RROOOM!

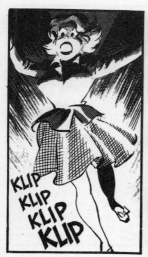

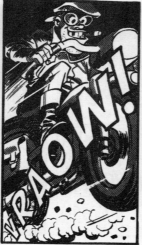

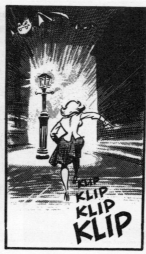

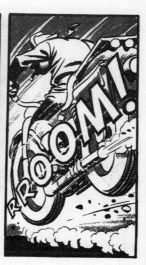

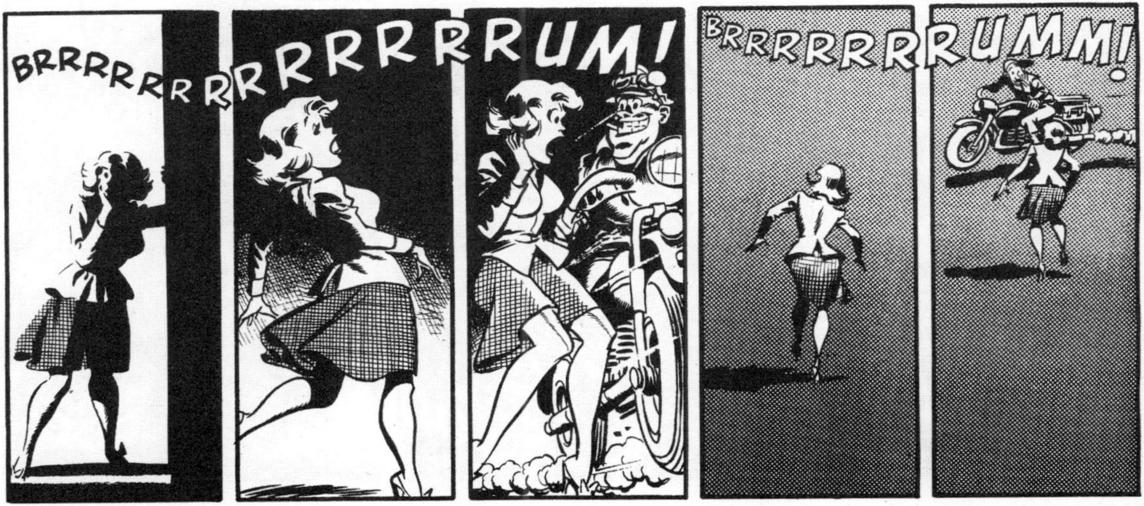
BRRRRRRRRRRRRRRRRUM!
BRRRRRRRRRUMM!

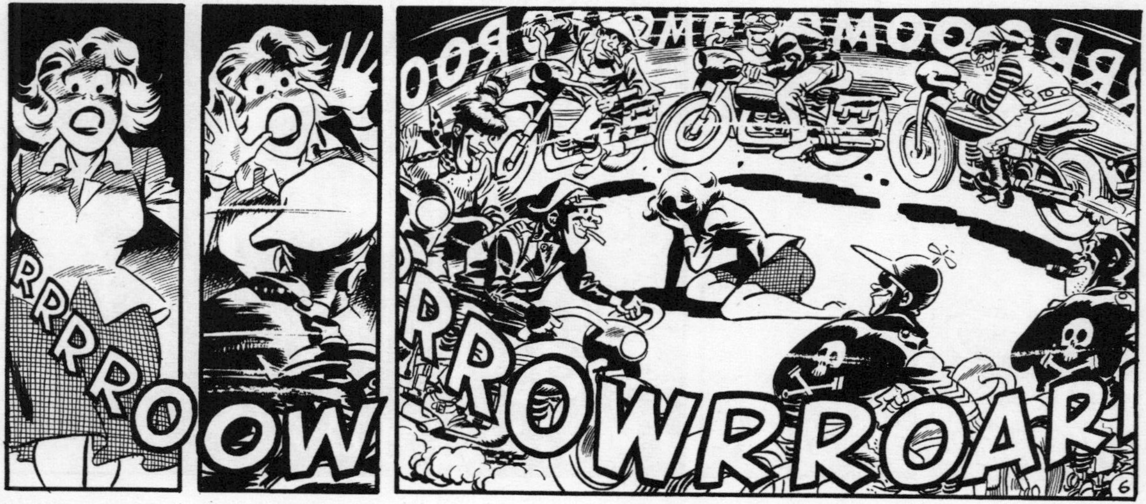
RRRROOOWRROWRROAR!

GRRR!
TRRUM
SKREE-E-E-E

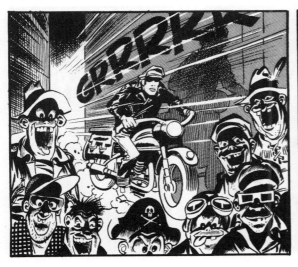

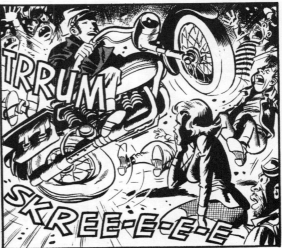

GET ON!
TRUM
TRUM
TRUM
GRRUMM
SPOK
KSPOK
KPAF
SIGH

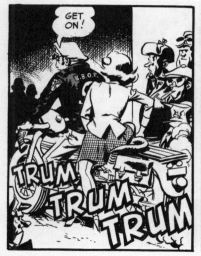

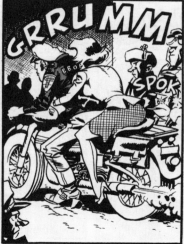

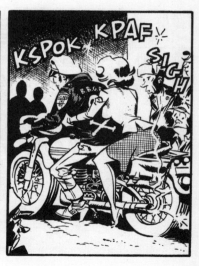

GOSH-DARN IT!
...OUT OF GAS!
... JUST AT MY BIG MOMENT... OUT OF GAS!
...JUST AS I'M ABOUT TO SAVE THE GIRL FROM THE VILLIANS LIKE A KNIGHT IN SHINING ARMOR...
...OUT OF GAS!
...SAVE THE GIRL FROM THE VILLIANS? WHATAYA MEAN, SAVE THE GIRL FROM THE VILLIANS? WE AIN'T VILLIANS! WE WERE JUST ABOUT TO GIVE HER THE TROPHY FOR THE MOTORCYCLE SPEED RECORD! SHE JUST WON IT... HANDS DOWN!
7

WEEEOOOAWWWWW
SLAM!!
SLAM! SLAM!
SLAM!
SLAM
COPS
PDQ
ALL RIGHT!... ALL RIGHT! WE HEARD SOME TROUBLE WAS GOING ON HERE! WE HEARD SOME MOTORCYCLE CRAZIES HAVE TAKEN OVER COSMOPOLIS! WE HEARD THEIR LEADER HATES COPS! WHERE IS HE?
...SHERIFF! WAIT A MINUTE! WAIT! WAIT!... THE MOTOR-CYCLE CRAZIES HAVE CHANGED!
...THEY BROKE INTO THE LAUNDRY... STOLE CLEAN CLOTHES AND THEY'VE CHANGED!
WANTED
FOR
CONTRAC
VIOLATIC

BUT THEN, JOHNNY, THE LEADER FELL IN LOVE WITH MY DAUGHTER! SHE CHANGED HIM!... HE DOESN'T LOOK FOR TROUBLE ANYMORE! THE TROUBLE'S RIGHT THERE WITH HIM AND HE DOESN'T HAVE TO LOOK!... HERE COMES JOHNNY NOW!
Schmekenheimer's SHOES
JOHNNY!... TELL THE SHERIFF HERE HOW YOU DON'T LOOK FOR TROUBLE ANY MORE!... TELL THE SHERIFF HOW YOU MET MY DAUGHTER AND FELL IN LOVE AND HOW THINGS ARE DIFFERENT NOW! ...WHATAYA SAY, JOHNNY, BWAH! ...WHATAYA SAY!
I HATE COPS!

...SOME POLICE-CHIEF YOU ARE! NOW THEY'RE RIDING AWAY!... IF YOU SHOW THEM KIND YOU'RE SCARED... THEY RUN ALL OVER YOU!... YOU MUSTN'T SHOW THEM YOU'RE SCARED!... YOU MUSTN'T LET 'EM SEE YOU'RE SCARED!... JUST LET ME GET UP...
...WAIT, SHERIFF! WAIT WAIT! THINGS ARE DIFFERENT!... DON'T GET UP TO ARREST THEM 'CAUSE YOU'LL SEE IN A MINUTE THINGS ARE DIFFERENT AND THEY'VE CHANGED!
WOOD
...WHO'S GETTING UP TO ARREST THEM? I'M GETTING UP TO GET OUT OF HERE SINCE I DON'T WANT TO LET 'EM SEE I'M SCARED!
...YES!... THE MOTORCYCLE CRAZIES ARE NOW BICYCLE CRAZIES!
...YOUTH HOSTEL... FORWARD!
...HEY! WAIT A MINUTE!... THEY REALLY HAVE CHANGED!
8

CARTOON DIGEST

SON OF MAD brings you a digest of the leading comic strips. We realize that the most popular part of the newspaper is the comics section. Therefore, in the interest of creating a better informed public, we have prepared this compact digest of the best of the comic sections. In other words, from now on you don't have to buy any newspapers...because these two pages condense the most popular parts of all the new newspapers and mainly saving you money.

Some idea, hey...you better informed, no-good, cheapskate public?

There's only one trouble...

We had to print the comic strips this way because of the page size.

So do not hold the page this way while reading comics.

Hold it this way.

Hey! what's wrong with your eyeballs?

LITTLE ORPHAN MELVIN

WELL SANDLE, HERE WE ARE WALKIN' DOWN THE OPEN ROAD SPEAKIN' PROFOUND PHILOSOPHICAL THOUGHTS. YES, SIR— THOSE WHO LIVE IN GLASS HOUSES, SHOULDN'T THROW BRICKS, AN' ON THE OTHER HAND—THE BETTER PART OF VALOR IS DESCRETION.

ARF!

I'M GLAD YOU SAID THAT, SANDLE—WHICH BRINGS TO MIND THAT— THERE CAN BE NO HIGH CIVILITY WITHOUT A DEEP MORALITY. ON THE OTHER HAND— WHAT IS FULLY UNDERSTOOD IS NOT POSSESSED.

ARF!

PRECISELY, SANDLE! FURTHERMORE— THOUGHT IS THE PROPERTY OF THOSE ONLY WHO CAN ENTERTAIN IT, THEN AGAIN— WAR IS HELL.

DID YOU GET ALL THAT DOWN, PUNJOKE?

½

YES, SAHIB DADDY PEACEBUCKS... BUT WHY DO YOU HAVE ME TAKING SHORTHAND OF WHAT LITTLE MISSY IS SAYING?

WHY INDEED! TO SEND TO THE 'BRIGHT SAYINGS' DEPARTMENTS OF THE NEWSPAPERS!

HOW DO YOU THINK I MAKE MY LIVING, YOU FOOL!

METT AND JUFF

BY " "

Panel 1:
SAY, JUFF... DON'T YOU THINK THAT YOUR APPEARANCE IS BECOMING A BIT DATED WITH THE HIGH HAT AND SIDEBURNS?

ADLER ELEVATED SNEAKERS

ER TED

Panel 2:
SURE, METT. BUT THE WORST PART IS, CONSTANTLY WEARING THESE WHITE GLOVES WITH THE ROLLED CUFFS WITH THE LINES ON THE BACK!

HEY SKINNY! PUT ON SOME FLESH!

CHARL ATLAS GYM - BUILD UP THOSE DORMANT MUSCLES

Panel 3:
SAY, JUTT... WHY DON'T WE TAKE THEM OFF!

GOOD IDEA, MEFF! ...GEE.... I WONDER WHAT OUR HANDS LOOK LIKE?

ADLER ELEVATED SNEAKERS

Panel 4:
GOSH! WHITE HANDS WITH ROLLED WRISTS WITH LINES ON THE BACK!

OUR HANDS TOO!

155

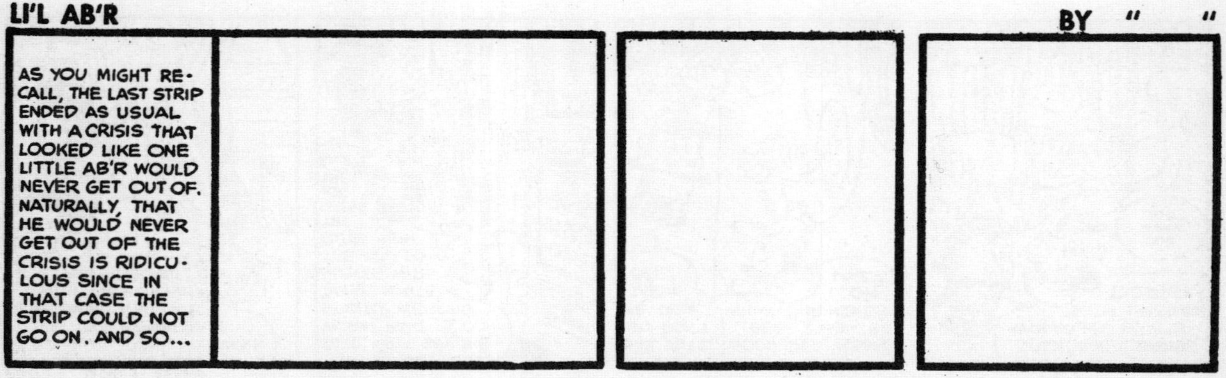
LI'L AB'R
BY " "
AS YOU MIGHT RE-CALL, THE LAST STRIP ENDED AS USUAL WITH A CRISIS THAT LOOKED LIKE ONE LITTLE AB'R WOULD NEVER GET OUT OF. NATURALLY, THAT HE WOULD NEVER GET OUT OF THE CRISIS IS RIDICU-LOUS SINCE IN THAT CASE THE STRIP COULD NOT GO ON. AND SO...

R. MORGAN, MD.

HMMM...STUDYING HIS PATIENT... WHETHER TO AFFECT PROPER PROGNOSIS BY ATTACKING THE ZYGOMATICUS OR THE GLUTEUS MAXIMUS PUZZLES ME!

WOULD A GOOD PUNCH IN THE ZYGOMATI- CUS MAKE HIM PAY HIS BILLS?

WAIT A MINUTE!

WAIT A MINUTE!

THIS HERE IS "Rx MORGAN MD," NOT "MEDICAL"!

MOVE THE T.V. CAMERAS, BOYS. WE'RE IN THE WRONG PLACE!

MY LAND! WITH ALL THESE 'DOCTOR' SHOWS IT SURE DO GET CONFUSING!

STARCHIE BY " "

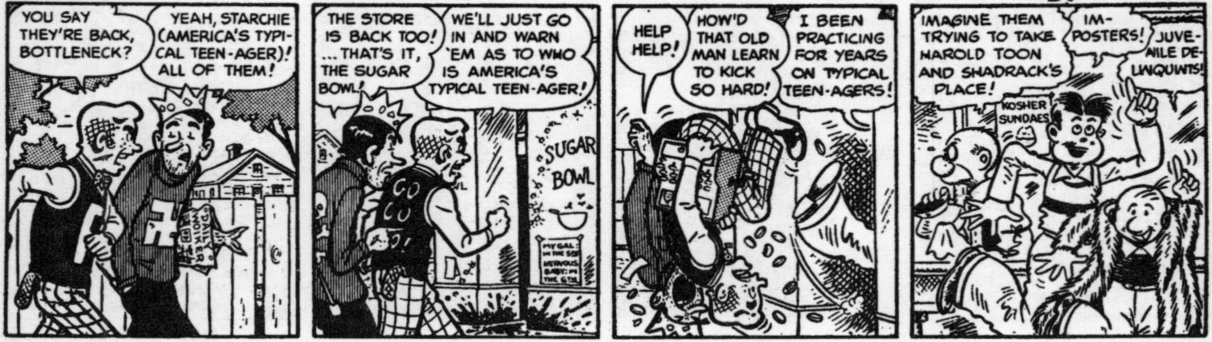
YOU SAY THEY'RE BACK, BOTTLENECK?
YEAH, STARCHIE (AMERICA'S TYPICAL TEEN-AGER)! ALL OF THEM!
DAILY WOIKER
THE STORE IS BACK TOO! ...THAT'S IT, THE SUGAR BOWL!
WE'LL JUST GO IN AND WARN 'EM AS TO WHO IS AMERICA'S TYPICAL TEEN-AGER!
SUGAR BOWL
HELP HELP!
HOW'D THAT OLD MAN LEARN TO KICK SO HARD!
I BEEN PRACTICING FOR YEARS ON TYPICAL TEEN-AGERS!
IMAGINE THEM TRYING TO TAKE HAROLD TOON AND SHADRACK'S PLACE!
IM-POSTERS!
JUVE-NILE DE-LINQUINTS!
KOSHER SUNDAES

POOPEYE

POOPEYE! WAIT! ARENT YOU RUNNING IN THAT DIRECTION BECAUSE THERE'S TROUBLE ABOUT AND YOU ALWAYS FIGHT TROUBLE AND EVIL, RIGHT?

RIGHT!

WAIT, POOPEYE! AREN'T YOU RUNNING IN THAT DIRECTION BECAUSE THERE'S SOME KIND OF SEA ADVENTURE STARTING AND YOU ALWAYS RUN TO FIGHT IN SEA ADVENTURES, RIGHT?

RIGHT!

BUT WAIT, POOPEYE! AREN'T YOU RUNNING IN THAT DIRECTION BECAUSE THERE'S A FOUL PLAY ON THE WATERFRONT AND YOU ALWAYS RUN TO FIGHT WATERFRONT FOUL PLAY, RIGHT?

RIGHT!

GO ON, TERRY KID! LEAN ON 'EM A LITTLE!

WELL THAT'S THE WRONG DIRECTION!

WELL THAT'S THE WRONG WATERFRONT!

159

CRIME DEPT. II: COME AWAY FROM YOUR FRESH PAINT HOMES ON TREE-LINED STREETS! . . . AWAY FROM YOUR CLEAN LINEN, YOUR GRADE-A MILK! COME TO THE GARBAGE-CANNED, BROKEN WINDOWED LAND OF THE UNDERWORLD! COME TO THE HOME OF THE GANGSTERS, GORILLAS, AND . . .

GANEFS!

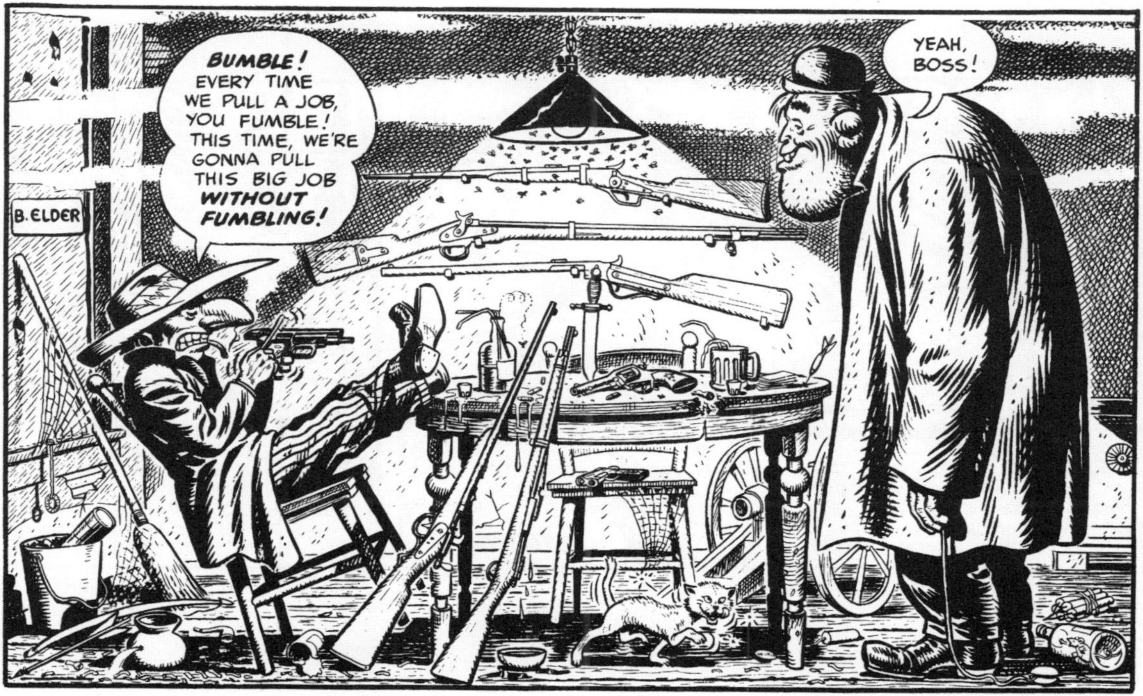
B. ELDER
BUMBLE! EVERY TIME WE PULL A JOB, YOU FUMBLE! THIS TIME, WE'RE GONNA PULL THIS BIG JOB WITHOUT FUMBLING!
YEAH, BOSS!

...EVERYTHING SET?... HUH? ARTILLERY OILED?... BULLETS SHINED UP?... SHOULDER HOLSTERS POLISHED AND DUBBINED?... GETAWAY CAR FIXED UP WITH FALSE LICENSE PLATES? HUH, BUMBLE?... HUH? HUH?
YEAH, BOSS!
SHUDDUP!
YOU TALK TOO MUCH!
SLAP
CRAK
FLAP FLAP
ALL RIGHT, BUMBLE! NOW LET'S GO THROUGH THIS THING ONCE MORE! HOW ARE WE GOING TO PULL THIS JOB?
YEAH, BOSS!
1

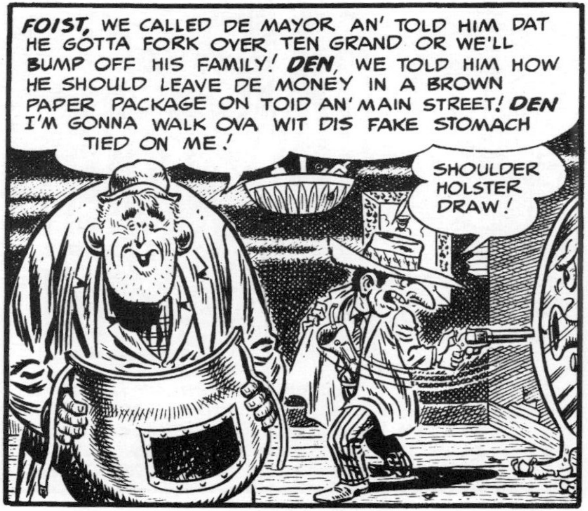
FOIST, WE CALLED DE MAYOR AN' TOLD HIM DAT HE GOTTA FORK OVER TEN GRAND OR WE'LL BUMP OFF HIS FAMILY! DEN, WE TOLD HIM HOW HE SHOULD LEAVE DE MONEY IN A BROWN PAPER PACKAGE ON TOID AN' MAIN STREET! DEN I'M GONNA WALK OVA WIT DIS FAKE STOMACH TIED ON ME!
SHOULDER HOLSTER DRAW!

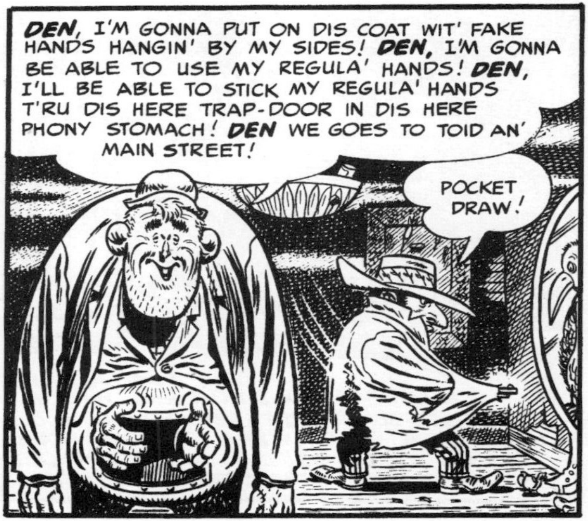
DEN, I'M GONNA PUT ON DIS COAT WIT' FAKE HANDS HANGIN' BY MY SIDES! DEN, I'M GONNA BE ABLE TO USE MY REGULA' HANDS! DEN, I'LL BE ABLE TO STICK MY REGULA' HANDS T'RU DIS HERE TRAP-DOOR IN DIS HERE PHONY STOMACH! DEN WE GOES TO TOID AN' MAIN STREET!
POCKET DRAW!

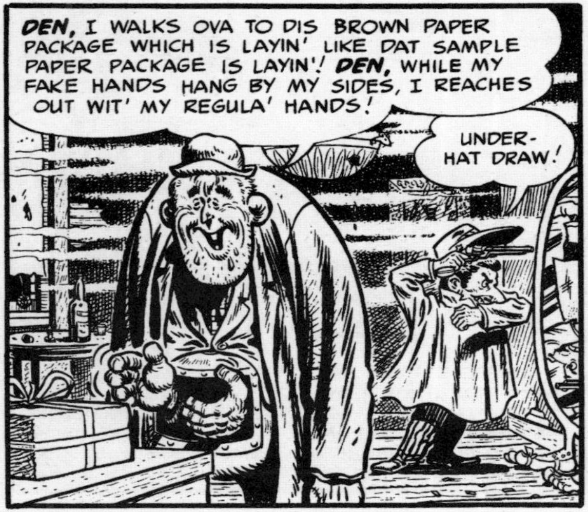
DEN, I WALKS OVA TO DIS BROWN PAPER PACKAGE WHICH IS LAYIN' LIKE DAT SAMPLE PAPER PACKAGE IS LAYIN'! DEN, WHILE MY FAKE HANDS HANG BY MY SIDES, I REACHES OUT WIT' MY REGULA' HANDS!
UNDER-HAT DRAW!

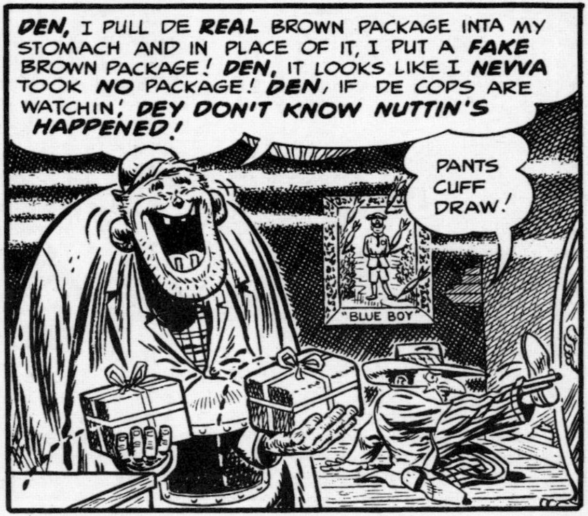
DEN, I PULL DE REAL BROWN PACKAGE INTA MY STOMACH AND IN PLACE OF IT, I PUT A FAKE BROWN PACKAGE! DEN, IT LOOKS LIKE I NEVVA TOOK NO PACKAGE! DEN, IF DE COPS ARE WATCHIN', DEY DON'T KNOW NUTTIN'S HAPPENED!
PANTS CUFF DRAW!
"BLUE BOY"

DEN DEY WATCH AN' DEY WATCH... AN DEN DEY GET TIRED AN' TAKE HOME DE FAKE PACKAGE... WHICH DEY TINK IS DE REAL PACKAGE! DEN WHEN DEY OPEN IT, INSTEAD OF DEIR MONEY, DEY FIND A STINK BOMB!
A STINK BOMB!
WHAT A GAG!
HEEE
YAA
HA HA HA HA HA HO HO HO
SHADDAP! THE TIME HAS COME! SYN-CHRONISE YOUR WATCHES! 8... 7... 6... 5... 4... 3... 2... 1... HACK! LET'S GO!
SMAK! SMAK!
2

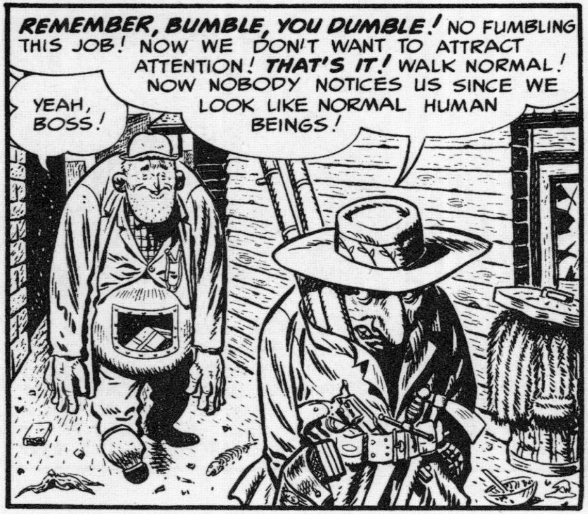
REMEMBER, BUMBLE, YOU DUMBLE! NO FUMBLING THIS JOB! NOW WE DON'T WANT TO ATTRACT ATTENTION! THAT'S IT! WALK NORMAL! NOW NOBODY NOTICES US SINCE WE LOOK LIKE NORMAL HUMAN BEINGS!
YEAH, BOSS!

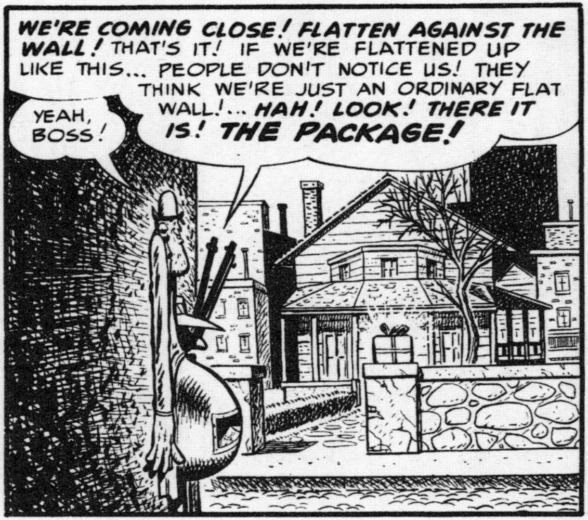
WE'RE COMING CLOSE! FLATTEN AGAINST THE WALL! THAT'S IT! IF WE'RE FLATTENED UP LIKE THIS... PEOPLE DON'T NOTICE US! THEY THINK WE'RE JUST AN ORDINARY FLAT WALL!... HAH! LOOK! THERE IT IS! THE PACKAGE!
YEAH, BOSS!

WALK NATURAL! ACT UNCON-CERNED! NOT TOO FAST! LA... LOO... LA
TWEE TWEE
LA... LEE... LA... LOO! TAKE IT EASY! TAKE IT EASY! WALK O-VER TO THE PA-A-ACKAGE
TWEE TWEE
YEAH, BOSS!
SHUDDAP!
LALEE LOO! HOW MANY TIMES I TOLD YOU NOT TO MENTION MY-HI NAME! LA... LOO!
SLAP! SLAP!
TWEE TWEE

LEE...LI...LO! DON'T FUMBLE! DO-O-O-N'T FUM-BLE! GET THE PACKAGE! LA-LEE...LI LO!
LI... LEE...LO! CLUM-SY I-DIOT! NOW TAKE IT E-EASY! NICE AND SLOW! LA...LEE...LOO! TAKE IT EA...
TWEE
FWEEE!
3

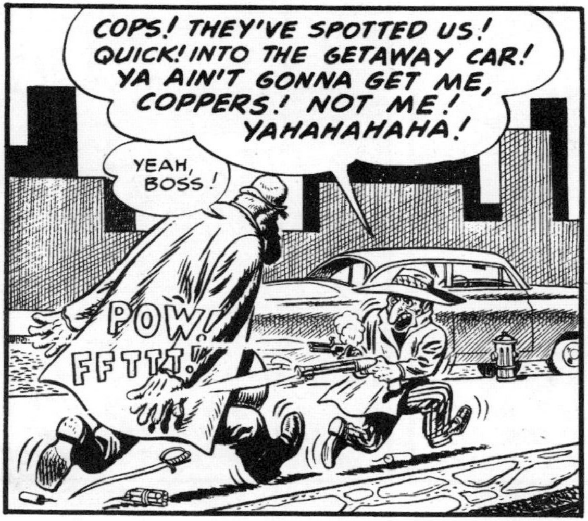
COPS! THEY'VE SPOTTED US! QUICK! INTO THE GETAWAY CAR! YA AIN'T GONNA GET ME, COPPERS! NOT ME! YAHAHAHAHA!
YEAH, BOSS!
POW!
FFTTT!

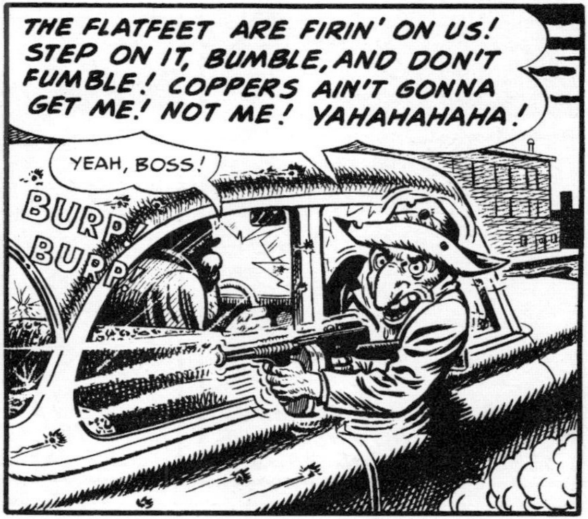
THE FLATFEET ARE FIRIN' ON US! STEP ON IT, BUMBLE, AND DON'T FUMBLE! COPPERS AIN'T GONNA GET ME! NOT ME! YAHAHAHAHA!
YEAH, BOSS!
BURP!
BURP!

THEY'VE SHOT THE ROOF OFF! BUT THEY AIN'T GONNA GET ME!
YEAH, BOSS!
BRAMMMMMM
THEY'VE SHOT THE SIDE OFF! BUT THEY AIN'T GONNA GET ME!
YEAH, BOSS!
BRAMMMM
THEY'VE SHOT THE OTHER SIDE OFF! BUT THEY AIN'T GONNA GET ME!
YEAH, BOSS!
BRRAM AM

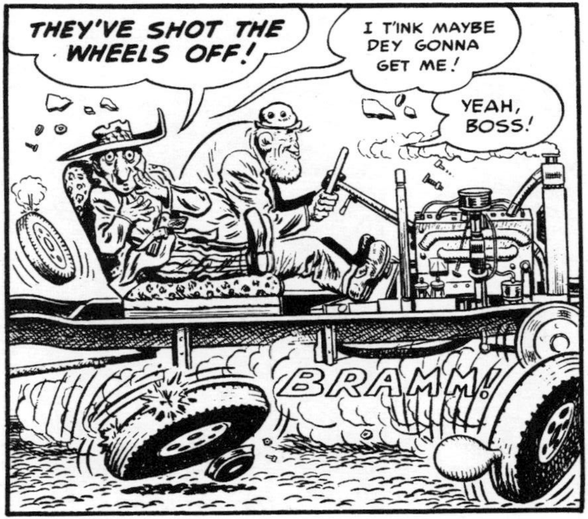
THEY'VE SHOT THE WHEELS OFF!
I T'INK MAYBE DEY GONNA GET ME!
YEAH, BOSS!
BRAMM!

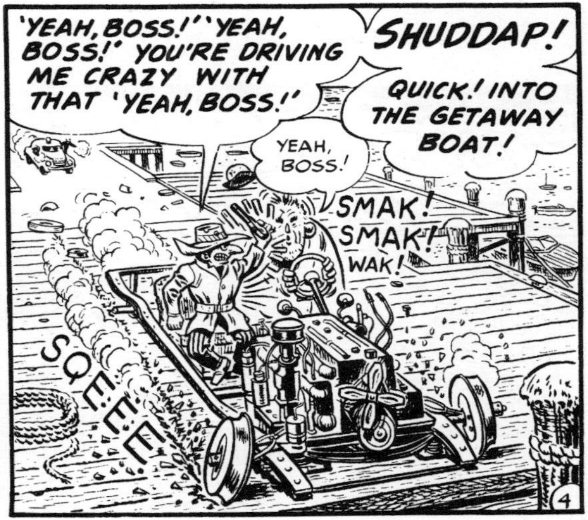
'YEAH, BOSS!' 'YEAH, BOSS!' YOU'RE DRIVING ME CRAZY WITH THAT 'YEAH, BOSS!'
SHUDDAP!
QUICK! INTO THE GETAWAY BOAT!
YEAH, BOSS!
SMAK! SMAK! WAK!
SQEEE
4

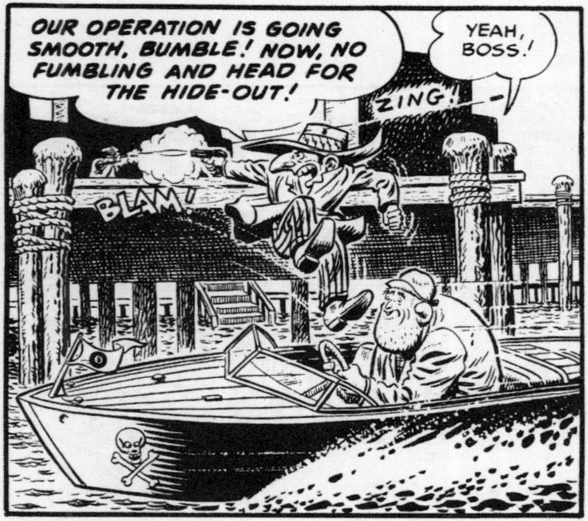
OUR OPERATION IS GOING SMOOTH, BUMBLE! NOW, NO FUMBLING AND HEAD FOR THE HIDE-OUT!
YEAH, BOSS!
ZING!
BLAM!

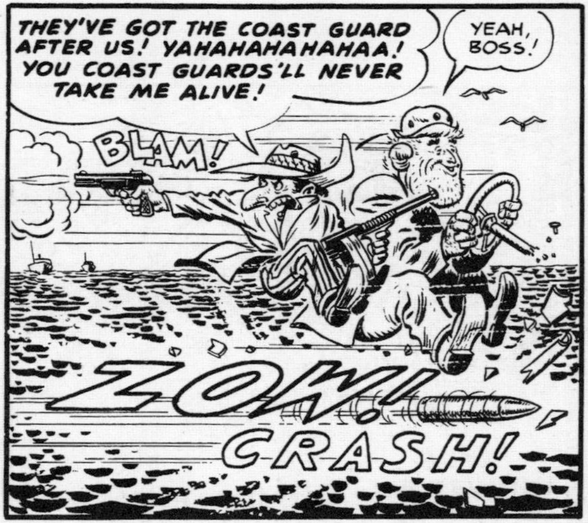
THEY'VE GOT THE COAST GUARD AFTER US! YAHAHAHAHAHAA! YOU COAST GUARDS'LL NEVER TAKE ME ALIVE!
YEAH, BOSS!
BLAM!
ZOW!
CRASH!

DIS IS A GOOD IDEA, BOSS... BREATHING T'ROUGH OUR GUN BARRELS!
SHUDDAP!
SLAP! SLAP! SLAP!
WELL! THEY'VE LOST US! NOW THERE'S JUST YOU AND ME AND THE TEN GRAND! RIGHT, BUMBLE? THERE! LET ME CARRY IT FOR A WHILE!
WE GONNA SPLIT IT UP, BOSS?
NOW, BOSS? HUH? HUH? NOW?
YEAH, BUMBLE! YOU FINALLY PULLED OFF THE BIG JOB WITH-OUT A FUMBLE! I'M INDEBTED TO YOU! I'M GONNA PAY YOU OFF!

YEAH, BOSS!
SNIFF! G-GOOD-BYE, BUMBLE! THIS HURTS YOU MORE THAN IT DOES ME... BUT THAT 'YEAH, BOSS' ROUTINE! IT'S DRIVING ME OUTTA MY MIND! 'YEAH, BOSS!' 'YEAH, BOSS!' 'YEAH, BOSS!'
RAT-TATATATAT!
Y... Y... YEAH... B...OSS...
GLUG!
AND NOW THE MONEY IS MINE! ALL MINE! AWAY! TO THE HIDE-OUT!
5

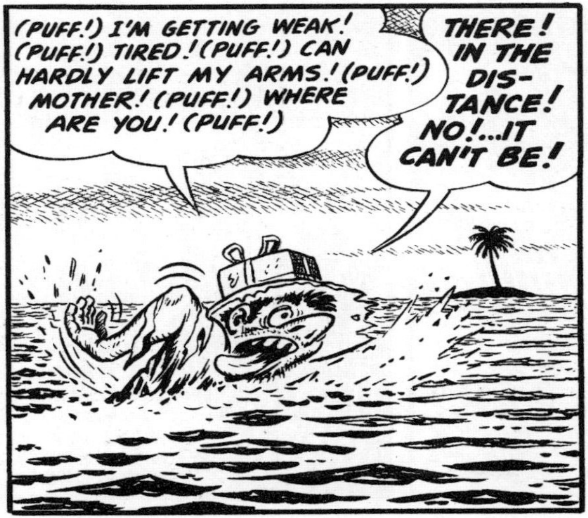
(PUFF!) I'M GETTING WEAK! (PUFF!) TIRED! (PUFF!) CAN HARDLY LIFT MY ARMS! (PUFF!) MOTHER! (PUFF!) WHERE ARE YOU! (PUFF!)
THERE! IN THE DIS-TANCE! NO!...IT CAN'T BE!

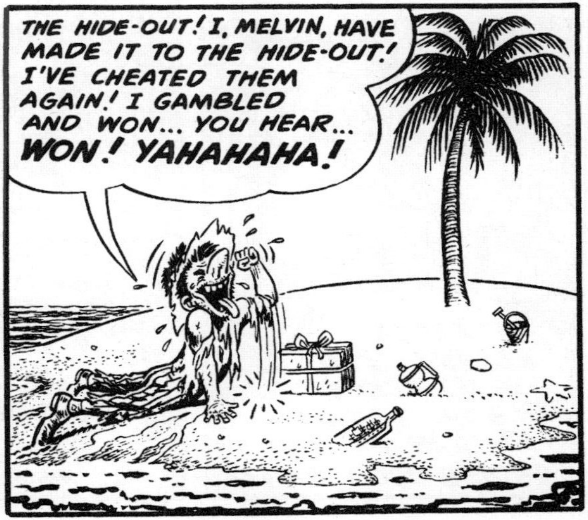
THE HIDE-OUT! I, MELVIN, HAVE MADE IT TO THE HIDE-OUT! I'VE CHEATED THEM AGAIN! I GAMBLED AND WON... YOU HEAR... WON! YAHAHAHA!

NOW... HIHIHIH... I CLIMB UP THE PALM TREE... HIHIHIHIH... WITH MY MONEY... HIHIHIHIH!
I CLIMB UP... HIHIHIH... TO THE HIDE-OUT SHACK... HIHIHIH... WITH THE SECRET COMBINATION... OPEN DOOR... HIHIHIH... GET INSIDE WITH MY MONEY!
KEEP OUT
LOCK DOOR BEHIND... HEE HEE HEE... OPEN PACKAGE... HEE HEE ... MONEY... HEE HEE... PRETTY MONEY...

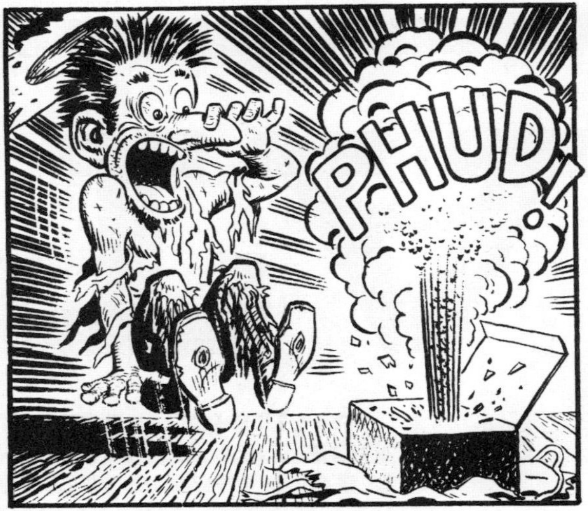
PHUD!

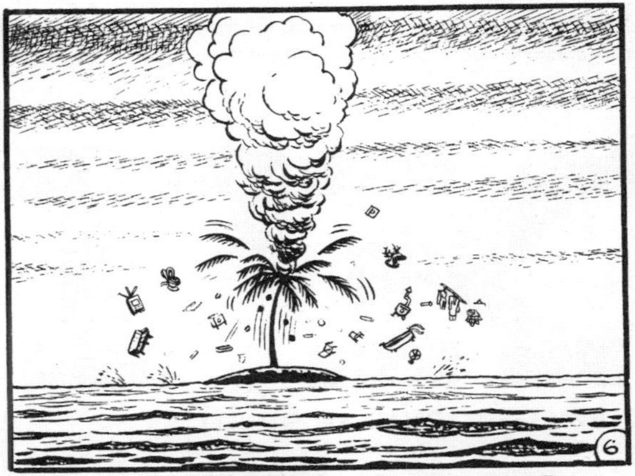

A FOUL STENCH OF A CELLULOID STINK BOMB RISES INTO THE CLEAR OCEAN AIR! FOR, YOU SEE...
BUMBLE... FUMBLED!

TALK DEPT.

SO . . . ONE RIDICULOUS ARTICLE FOLLOWS THE NEXT AND THE FOLLOWING ARTICLE CONCERNS

PICTURES BY WALLACE WOOD

TALK

You know how sometimes you look at people from a distance and as you watch, you imagine in your mind what they're saying. Like forinstance . . . there's the fancy dame with the high-class gent conversing in low tones in the cocktail lounge. Down below we show . . .

Next, we go back and start all over again. Once more we are sitting with beady eyes watching the fancy dame with the high-class gent conversing in low tones in the cocktail lounge. Only this time we have x-ray ears and we can hear every word. So down below is . . .

What it *looks* like they're saying

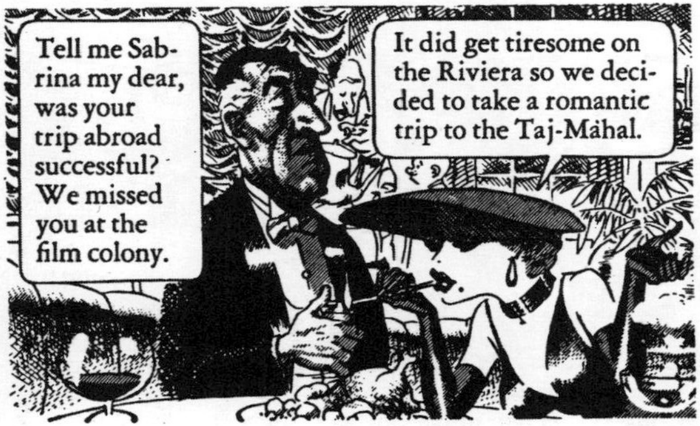
Tell me Sabrina my dear, was your trip abroad successful? We missed you at the film colony.
It did get tiresome on the Riviera so we decided to take a romantic trip to the Taj-Mahal.

What they *really* are saying . . .

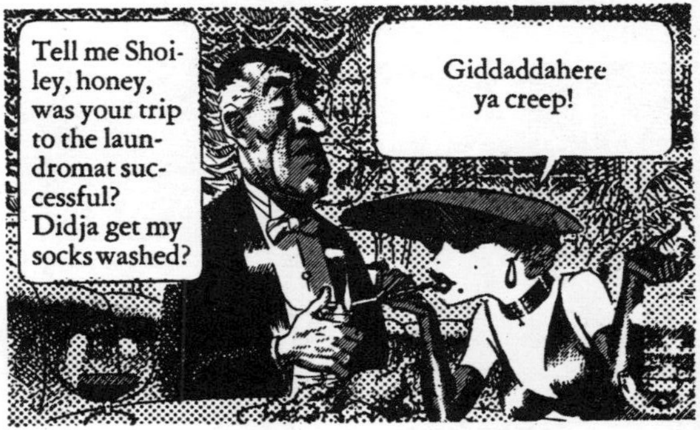
Tell me Shoiley, honey, was your trip to the laundromat successful? Didja get my socks washed?
Giddaddahere ya creep!

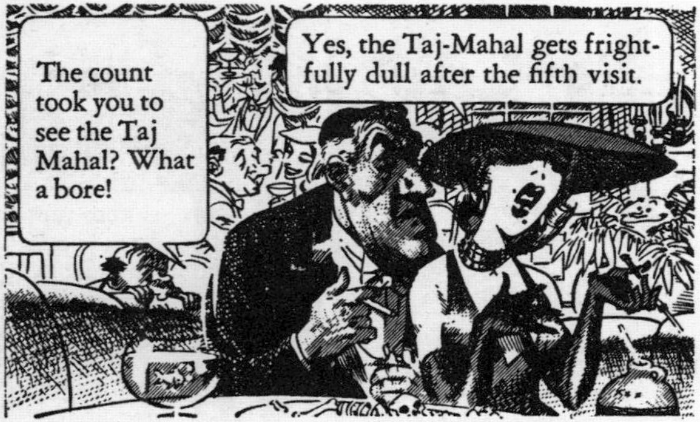
The count took you to see the Taj Mahal? What a bore!
Yes, the Taj-Mahal gets frightfully dull after the fifth visit.

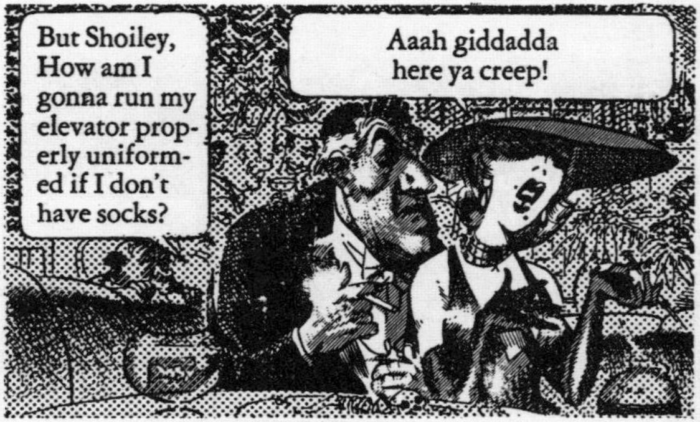
But Shoiley, How am I gonna run my elevator properly uniformed if I don't have socks?
Aaah giddadda here ya creep!

Do you get the idea? Is it beginning to jell? If not, read the page over carefully a couple more times. Memorize and take notes. Then turn the page for more . . .

How s about the graduation ceremony where the principal is seen to converse briefly with each nervous student as he (the principal) hands over the diploma . . .

What it *looks* like they're saying

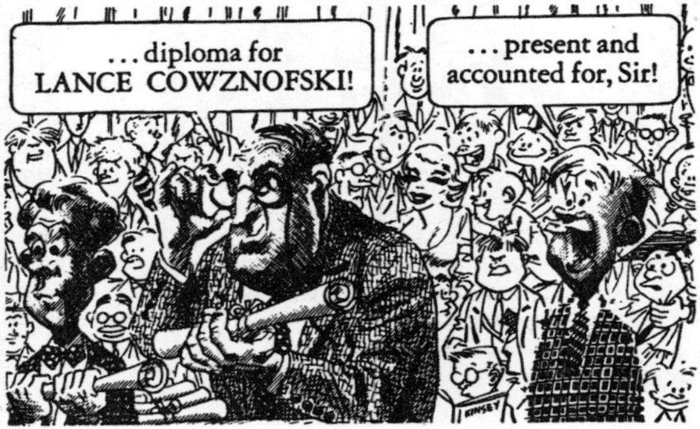

. . . diploma for LANCE COWZNOFSKI!
. . . present and accounted for, Sir!

What they *really* are saying . . .

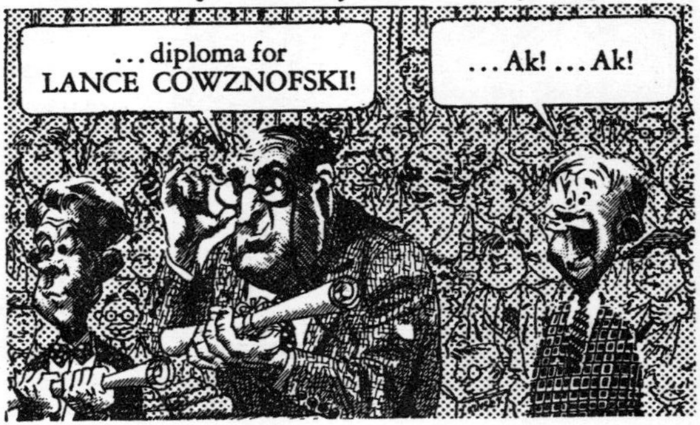

. . . diploma for LANCE COWZNOFSKI!
. . . Ak! . . . Ak!

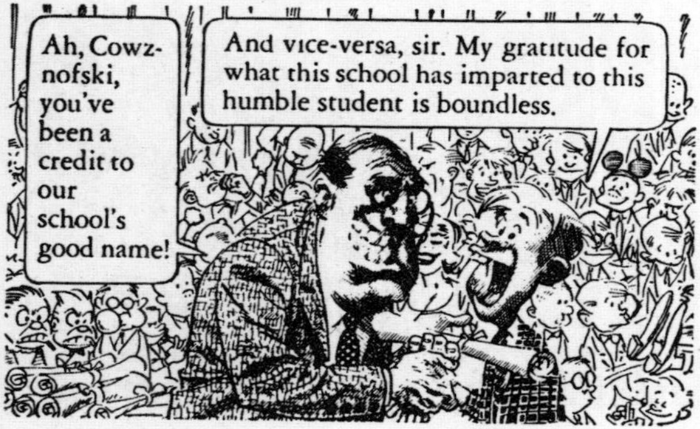
Ah, Cowznofski, you've been a credit to our school's good name!
And vice-versa, sir. My gratitude for what this school has imparted to this humble student is boundless.

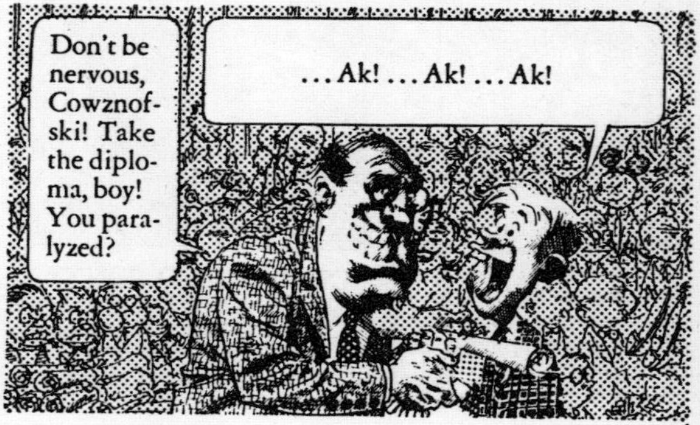
Don't be nervous, Cowznofski! Take the diploma, boy! You paralyzed?
...Ak!...Ak!...Ak!

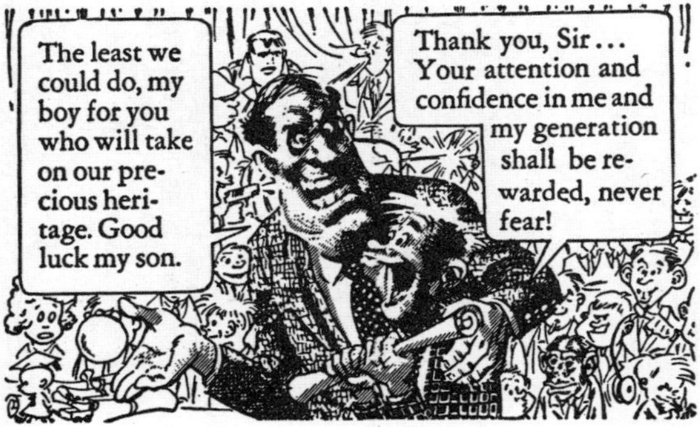
The least we could do, my boy for you who will take on our precious heritage. Good luck my son.
Thank you, Sir ... Your attention and confidence in me and my generation shall be rewarded, never fear!

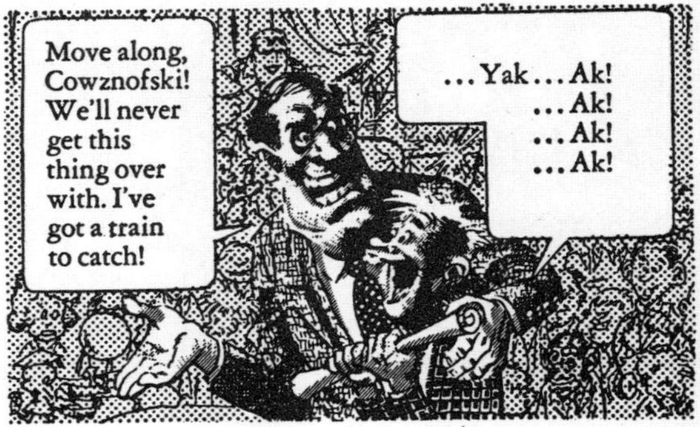
Move along, Cowznofski! We'll never get this thing over with. I've got a train to catch!
... Yak ... Ak!
... Ak!
... Ak!
... Ak!

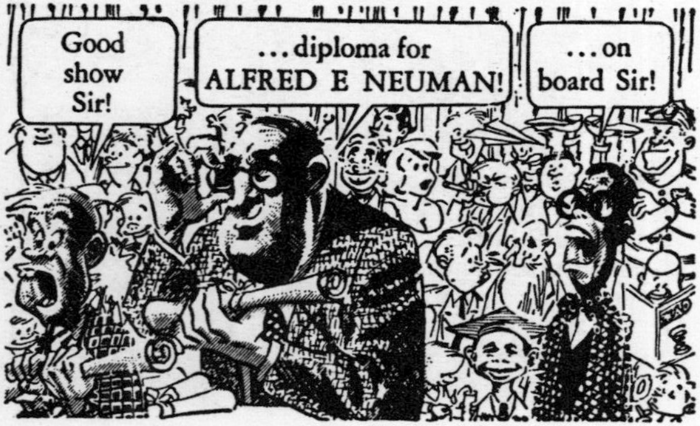
Good show Sir!
...diploma for ALFRED E NEUMAN!
...on board Sir!

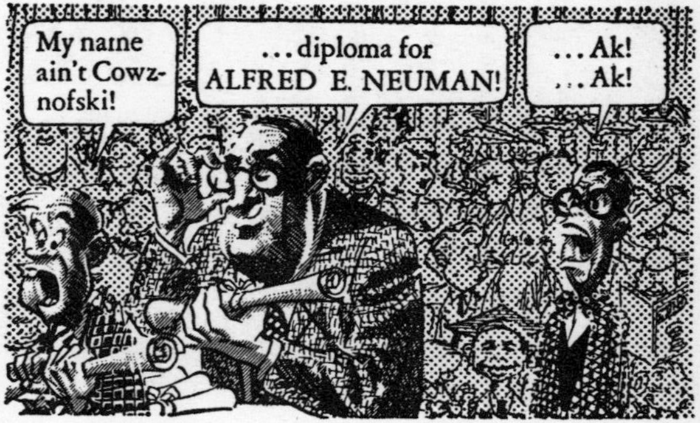
My name ain't Cowznofski!
...diploma for ALFRED E. NEUMAN!
...Ak! ...Ak!

There's the dance where miserable, inferior you are watching with your gimlet eyes the fast guy with the slick chick trading what seems to be snappy repartee.

What it *looks* like they're saying

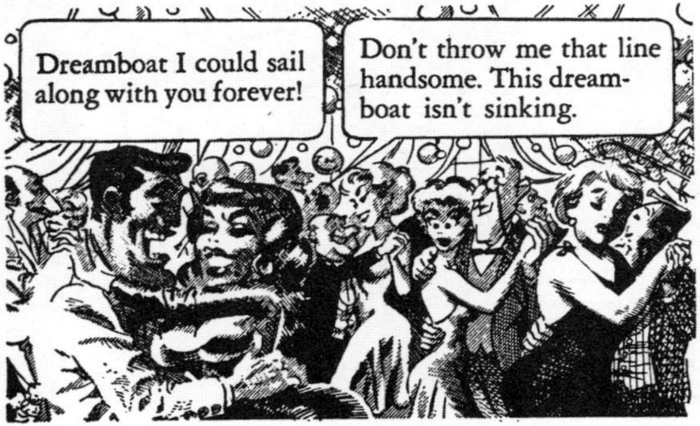
Dreamboat I could sail along with you forever!
Don't throw me that line handsome. This dream-boat isn't sinking.

What they *really* are saying . . .

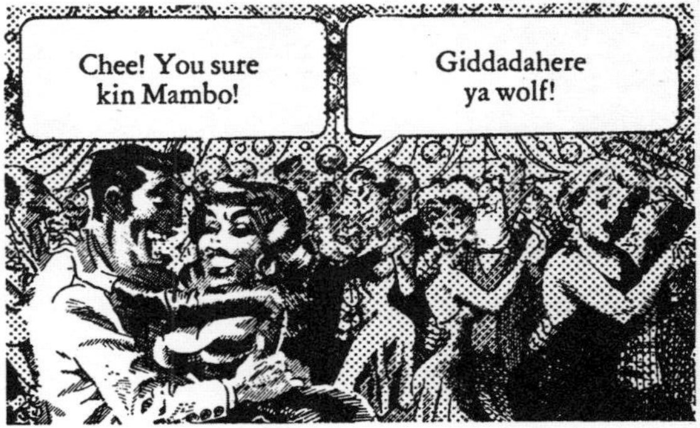
Chee! You sure kin Mambo!
Giddadahere ya wolf!

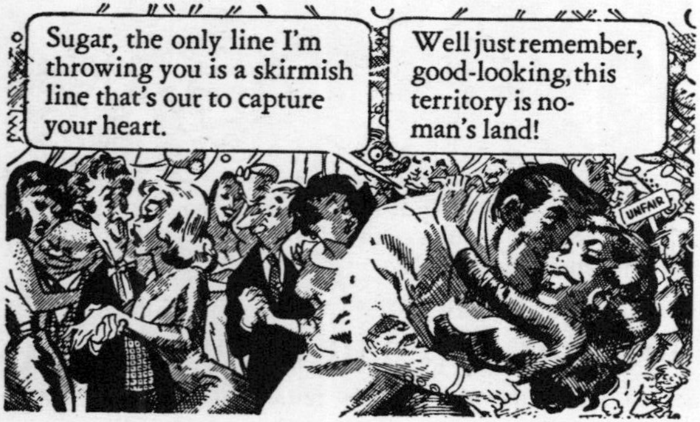
Sugar, the only line I'm throwing you is a skirmish line that's our to capture your heart.
Well just remember, good-looking, this territory is no-man's land!
UNFAIR

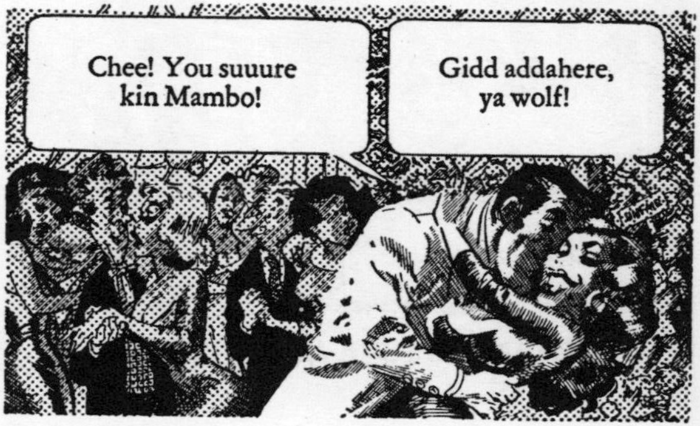
Chee! You suuure kin Mambo!
Gidd addahere, ya wolf!

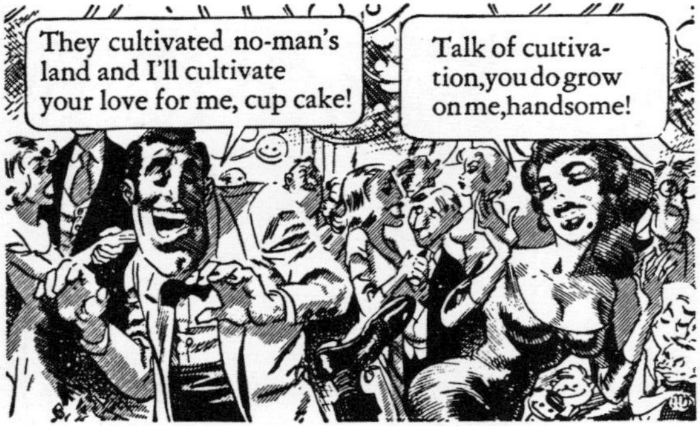
They cultivated no-man's land and I'll cultivate your love for me, cup cake!
Talk of cultivation, you do grow on me, handsome!

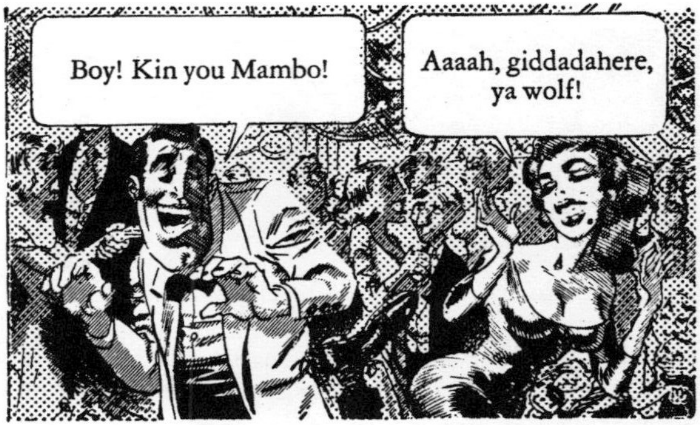
Boy! Kin you Mambo!
Aaaah, giddadahere, ya wolf!

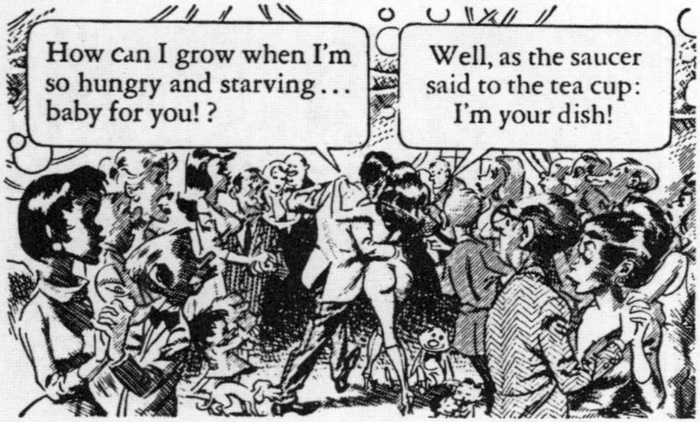
How can I grow when I'm so hungry and starving... baby for you! ?
Well, as the saucer said to the tea cup: I'm your dish!

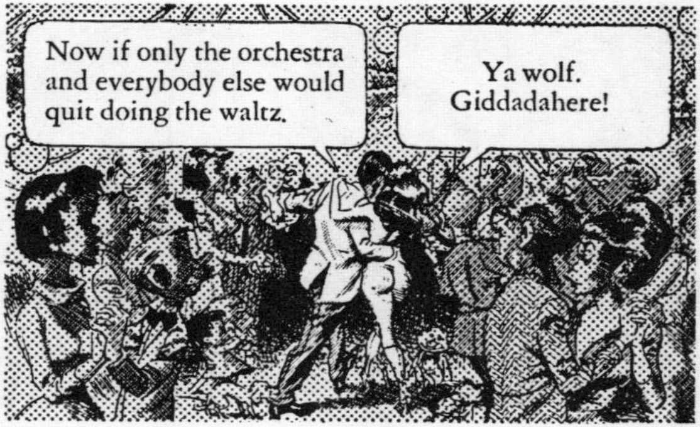
Now if only the orchestra and everybody else would quit doing the waltz.
Ya wolf. Giddadahere!

Then . . . there's that brief moment when the speaker finishes and turns to sit down amidst a seeming flurry of congratulations from his neighbors on the rostrum...

What it *looks* like they're saying

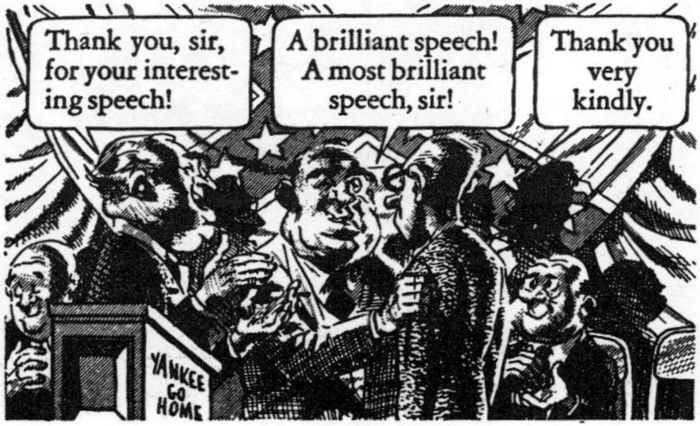
Thank you, sir, for your interesting speech!
A brilliant speech! A most brilliant speech, sir!
Thank you very kindly.
YANKEE GO HOME

What they *really* are saying...

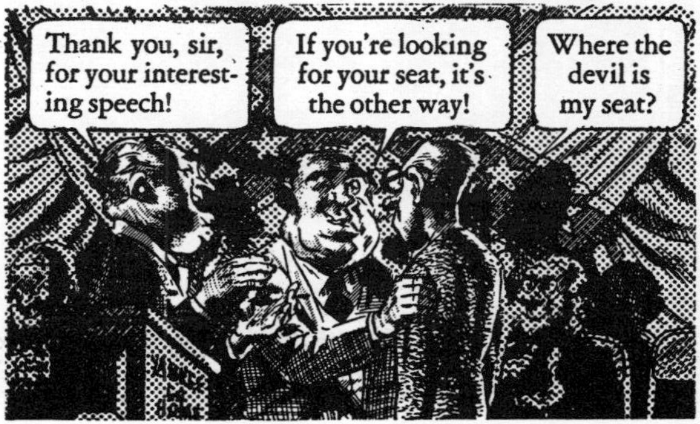
Thank you, sir, for your interesting speech!
If you're looking for your seat, it's the other way!
Where the devil is my seat?

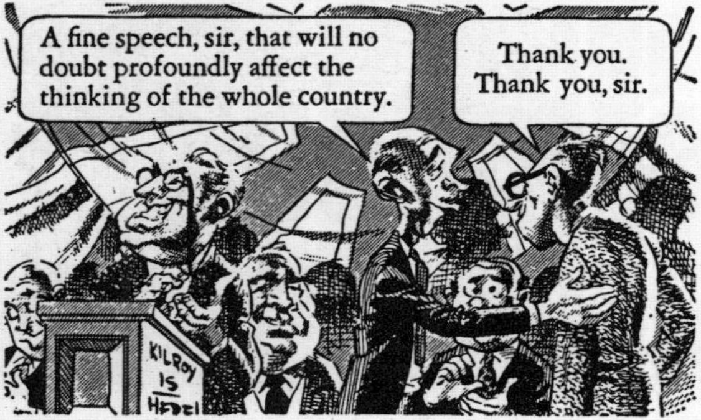
A fine speech, sir, that will no doubt profoundly affect the thinking of the whole country.
Thank you. Thank you, sir.
KILROY IS HERE!

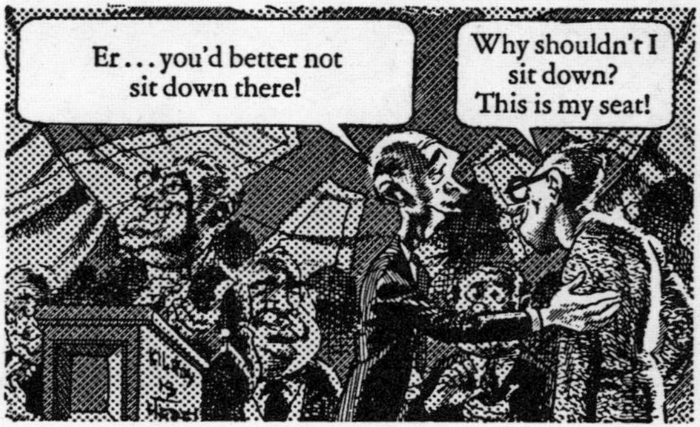
Er . . . you'd better not sit down there!
Why shouldn't I sit down? This is my seat!

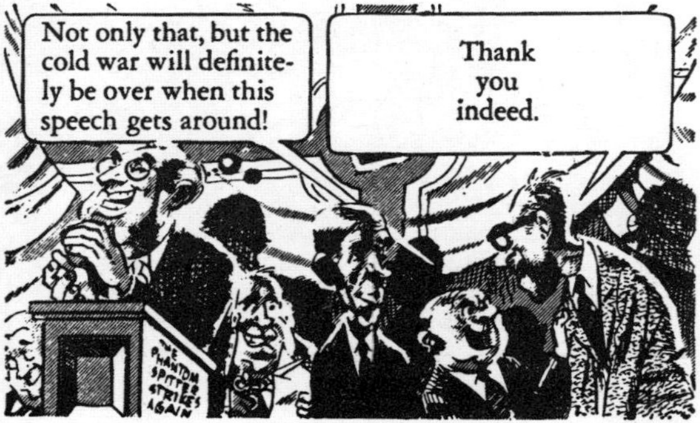
Not only that, but the cold war will definite-ly be over when this speech gets around!
Thank you indeed.
THE PHANTOM SPITTER STRIKES AGAIN

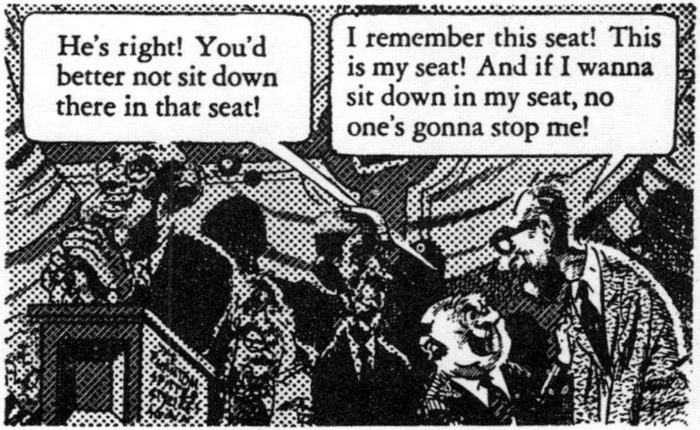
He's right! You'd better not sit down there in that seat!
I remember this seat! This is my seat! And if I wanna sit down in my seat, no one's gonna stop me!

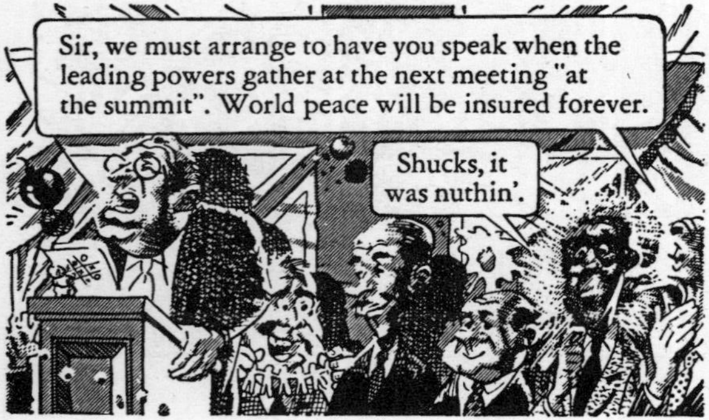
Sir, we must arrange to have you speak when the leading powers gather at the next meeting "at the summit". World peace will be insured forever.
Shucks, it was nuthin'.

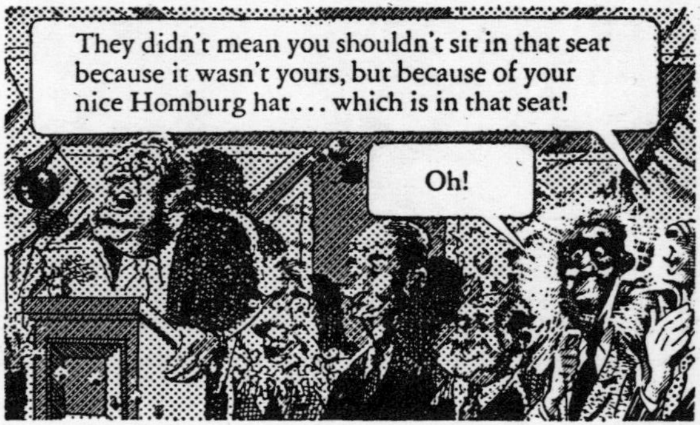
They didn't mean you shouldn't sit in that seat because it wasn't yours, but because of your nice Homburg hat . . . which is in that seat!
Oh!

END

Also available from ibooks:

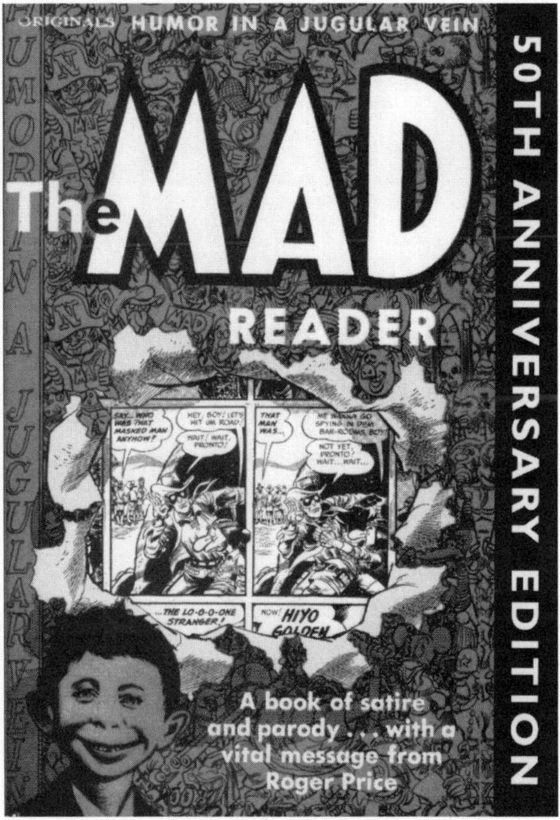
ORIGINALS
HUMOR IN A JUGULAR VEIN
The MAD READER
50TH ANNIVERSARY EDITION
SAY... HIYO WAS THAT MASKED MAN ANYHOW?
HEY, BOY! LET'S HIT UM ROAD!
THAT MAN WAS...
NOT YET, PRONTO! WAIT... WAIT...
...THE LO-O-O-ONE STRANGER!
NOW! HIYO GOLDEN
A book of satire and parody . . . with a vital message from Roger Price

The MAD Reader

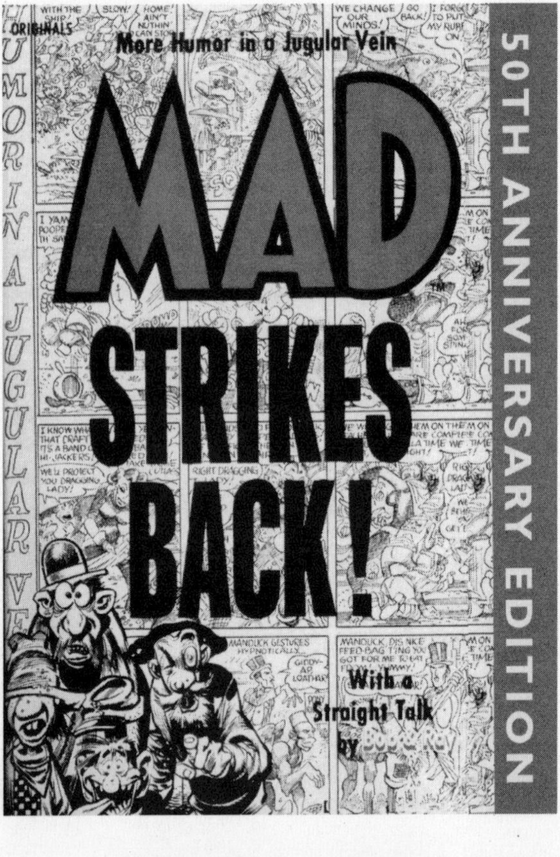
More Humor in a Jugular Vein
MAD
STRIKES BACK!
With a Straight Talk by
50TH ANNIVERSARY EDITION

MAD Strikes Back!

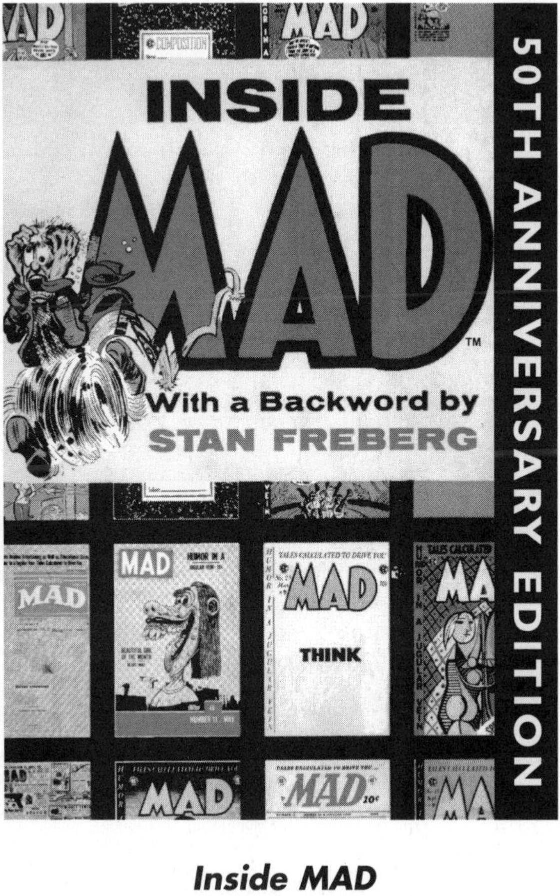
INSIDE
MAD™
With a Backword by
STAN FREBERG
50TH ANNIVERSARY EDITION

Inside MAD

BEER
William M. Gaines'
UTTERLY
MAD
TM
50TH ANNIVERSARY EDITION
4th Superb Collection!

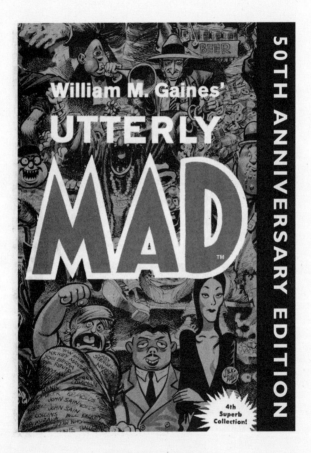

Utterly MAD

William M. Gaines'
THE BROTHERS
MAD
TM
50TH ANNIVERSARY EDITION
5 th
Superb
Collection!

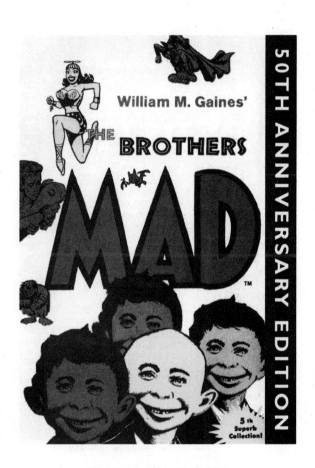

The Brothers MAD

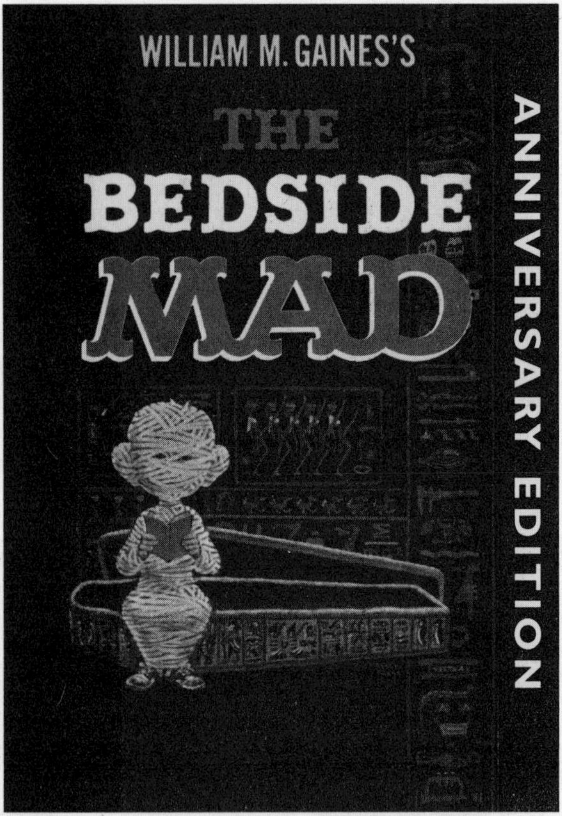
WILLIAM M. GAINES'S
THE
BEDSIDE
MAD
ANNIVERSARY EDITION

The Bedside MAD